THE MANY FACES OF JOY:

Happiness in Philosophy,

Religion, Literature and Art

THE MANY FACES OF JOY:

Happiness in Philosophy,

Religion, Literature and Art

Joyce Åkesson

Pallas Athena Distribution

Lund 2025

The Many Faces of Joy: *Happiness in Philosophy, Religion, Literature and Art*

By Joyce Åkesson

Book design by Pallas Athena Distribution

ISBN: 978-91-989454-2-3

ALSO BY JOYCE ÅKESSON

Abu Nuwas: Selected Poems of Love, Wine and Life, Pallas Athena Distribution, 2025.

The Philosophy of Love: Bridging Western, Eastern, and Arabic Thought, Pallas Athena Distribution, 2025.

A Dictionary of Economic and Business, English - Arabic, Pallas Athena Distribution, 2013.

Arabic Love Poetry from the Desert: Majnun Leyla, Arabic Text, Commentary and Translations, Pallas Athena Distribution, 2012.

Arabic Proverbs and Wise Sayings, Pallas Athena Distribution, 2011.

Love's Thrilling Dimensions, Pallas Athena Distribution, 2009.

The Invitation, Pallas Athena Distribution, 2009.

The Complexity of the Irregular Verbal and Nominal Forms & the Phonological Changes in Arabic, Pallas Athena Distribution, 2009.

Arabic Morphology and Phonology: Based on the Marāḥ al-Arwāḥ by Aḥmad b. ʿAlī b. Masʿūd, Studies in Semitic Languages and Linguistics, Brill Academic Publishers, 2001.

CONTENTS

Preface

Happiness is a rich, multi-dimensional concept that has intrigued humanity across centuries and cultures. It touches every facet of human existence and has been a focal point in disciplines ranging from religion and philosophy to psychology, literature, and art. This book aims to explore and develop the idea of happiness by delving into its various dimensions and examining how the pursuit of happiness manifests in different realms of human thought and experience.

One of the most consistent findings in research is the profound role that relationships play in fostering happiness. Strong, supportive social connections are among the most reliable predictors of long-term well-being, while loneliness and isolation can create significant barriers to achieving happiness. This suggests that nurturing relationships and cultivating community are essential for a fulfilling life.

Practical strategies to enhance happiness have gained considerable attention in psychological literature. Techniques such as mindfulness meditation encourage individuals to remain present and cultivate awareness of positive experiences. Similarly, practices like expressing gratitude can reframe one's perspective, drawing attention to the abundance and joy in everyday life.

The nature of happiness differs significantly across cultures. In Western societies, happiness is frequently linked to personal achievement, autonomy, and the fulfillment of individual desires. By contrast, Eastern traditions often emphasize collective harmony, spiritual growth, and the minimization of desires as pathways to contentment. This cultural variance underscores the diverse ways in which happiness can be understood and pursued.

Goal-setting also emerges as a central component of happiness. When individuals pursue goals aligned with their core values, they often experience a heightened sense of purpose and fulfillment. Interestingly, acts of altruism have been shown to boost happiness not only for recipients but also for those who engage in generous behaviors, reinforcing the interconnectedness of personal well-being and community care.

Another important dimension of happiness is resilience—the ability to adapt to life's inevitable changes and recover from setbacks. Sustained happiness often arises from this capacity to navigate adversity and maintain a sense of balance through life's ups and downs. However, research also highlights the phenomenon of hedonic adaptation, where individuals return to a baseline level of happiness even after significant positive or negative events. This underscores the importance of cultivating internal, enduring sources of happiness rather than relying solely on external circumstances.

Interestingly, the active pursuit of happiness can sometimes hinder its attainment. A relentless focus on achieving happiness may detract from the simple joy of living in the present moment. Thus, happiness often flourishes when it is approached indirectly, through engagement in meaningful activities and authentic connections.

As this book unfolds, I will explore how happiness has been conceptualized across diverse cultural, philosophical, and artistic traditions. In Western philosophy, the pursuit of happiness has long been intertwined with ideas of virtue, reason, and personal fulfillment. Thinkers from Aristotle to contemporary scholars have grappled with the nature of well-being and the factors that contribute to a flourishing life. Eastern philosophies, by contrast, often emphasize harmony, detachment, and the cultivation of inner peace as essential pathways to happiness. The teachings of Confucianism, Buddhism, and Daoism reveal nuanced understandings of contentment, impermanence, and the interconnectedness of all things.

Religious traditions, both ancient and contemporary, offer rich insights into the spiritual dimensions of happiness. Judaism emphasizes the importance of joy in fulfilling God's commandments and celebrating life's blessings. In Christianity, joy is frequently linked to faith, grace, and the love of God. Hinduism speaks of bliss as a state attainable through self-realization and alignment with the divine. Islamic teachings emphasize gratitude, patience, and the pursuit of righteous actions as avenues to true happiness. Across these varied traditions, the search for happiness is often seen not as a fleeting pleasure but as a deeper, more enduring state tied to purpose, transcendence, and connection with others.

Literature and art, too, reflect humanity's enduring quest for joy and meaning. From epic poetry to modern novels, stories have long served as mirrors of the human condition, capturing the trials and triumphs that shape our emotional lives. Visual art, music, and theater provide further dimensions to this exploration, offering symbolic representations of longing, fulfillment, and the beauty found in everyday existence. These creative expressions not only document the pursuit of happiness but also inspire and provoke reflection on what it means to live a meaningful life.

By weaving together these varied perspectives, this book seeks to illuminate the multifaceted nature of happiness. Through philosophical inquiry, spiritual reflection, and artistic interpretation, we will journey across cultures and centuries to uncover the timeless and universal threads that bind humanity in its shared aspiration for joy and fulfillment. It is my hope that readers will find valuable insights and practical tools to foster greater happiness in their own lives, in ways that resonate deeply with their unique journeys and aspirations.

Chapter I
Happiness in Western philosophy

Throughout history, philosophers have grappled with the concept of happiness and what it truly means to live a fulfilled life. From the ancient Greeks to modern thinkers, the pursuit of happiness has been a central theme in philosophical discourse. Understanding the historical perspectives on happiness can provide valuable insights into how different philosophical traditions have approached this fundamental human desire.

I.1 The Stoic philosophy of happiness

I.1.1 The Stoic definition of happiness

In the study of philosophy, one of the most enduring questions that has captivated the minds of thinkers throughout the ages is the nature of happiness. For students seeking to explore different philosophical perspectives on this topic, one particularly compelling viewpoint is that of the Stoics. Stoicism, founded by the ancient Greek philosopher Zeno of Citium (l. c. 336-265 BCE), emphasizes the importance of living in accordance with nature and developing a strong sense of moral integrity. The Stoic definition of happiness is rooted in the idea that true happiness can be achieved through the cultivation of inner strength and virtue, rather than through external circumstances.

According to the Stoics, happiness is not dependent on external factors such as wealth, fame, or pleasure. Instead, true happiness is found in living a life of virtue and in accordance with reason. This means cultivating qualities such as wisdom, courage, self-discipline, and justice, and living in harmony with the natural order of the universe.

In Stoic philosophy, the key to happiness lies in developing a mindset that is resilient in the face of adversity. By cultivating a sense of inner peace and tranquility, Stoics believe that individuals can find lasting happiness even in the midst of challenging circumstances. This resilience is achieved through practices such as mindfulness, self-reflection, and acceptance of things beyond our control.

For students interested in exploring the Stoic definition of happiness, it is important to understand that this philosophy is not about denying or suppressing emotions. Instead, Stoicism encourages individuals to cultivate a sense of emotional balance and equanimity, allowing them to navigate life's ups and downs with grace and resilience.

I.1.2 The role of virtue in Stoic happiness

According to Stoic teachings, true happiness is not found in external circumstances or material possessions, but rather in the cultivation of virtues such as wisdom, courage, justice, and temperance. By living a virtuous life, individuals can achieve a state of inner peace and tranquility that is not dependent on external factors.

Unlike Epicurean philosophy, which focuses on pursuing pleasure and avoiding pain, Stoicism teaches that happiness is not the result of indulging in fleeting pleasures, but rather in living a life of moral excellence. While Epicureans believe that happiness comes from seeking pleasure and avoiding pain, Stoics argue that true happiness comes from living a life of virtue and moral integrity.

I.1.3 Techniques for achieving Stoic happiness

In the pursuit of happiness, Stoicism offers valuable techniques that students can incorporate into their daily lives to achieve a sense of contentment and fulfillment. One of the key techniques for achieving stoic happiness is practicing mindfulness. By being present in the moment and accepting things as they come, students can cultivate a sense of inner peace that is not dependent on external circumstances.

Another important technique for achieving stoic happiness is practicing gratitude. In a world where we are constantly bombarded with messages of lack and scarcity, taking the time to appreciate the blessings in our lives can shift our perspective and help us find joy in the simple things. By focusing on what we have rather than what we lack, we can cultivate a sense of abundance and fulfillment.

Stoicism also emphasizes the importance of self-discipline and self-control in achieving happiness. By practicing moderation and restraint in our actions and emotions, we can avoid being swept away by impulses and desires that ultimately lead to unhappiness. Students can benefit from setting clear boundaries and sticking to them, whether it be in their studies, relationships, or personal habits.

Furthermore, Stoicism encourages students to cultivate a sense of resilience in the face of adversity. By recognizing that challenges and setbacks are a natural part of life, students can learn to accept them with grace and fortitude. Rather than being overwhelmed by difficulties, students can see them as opportunities for growth and self-improvement.

I.2 The Epicurean philosophy of happiness

I.2.1 The Epicurean concept of happiness

In the pursuit of happiness, one particular school of thought that students may find intriguing is the Epicurean concept of happiness. Epicurus, a Greek philosopher who lived in the 4th century BC, believed that true happiness could be achieved through the pursuit of pleasure and the avoidance of pain. However, it is important to note that Epicurus' understanding of pleasure went beyond mere physical indulgence; he believed that true happiness came from living a life of moderation and tranquility.

Epicurus argued that the key to happiness was to free oneself from unnecessary desires and fears, as these were the main sources of pain and anxiety. By focusing on simple pleasures, such as friendship, freedom, and intellectual pursuits, one could achieve a state of contentment and peace. Epicurus believed that true happiness could only be attained by living in harmony with nature and by cultivating a sense of inner tranquility.

Unlike the Stoics, who believed in self-discipline and self-control as the path to happiness, Epicurus emphasized the importance of pleasure as a means to achieving a good life. However, it is important to note that Epicurus' concept of pleasure was not hedonistic or selfish; rather, he believed that true pleasure came from living a virtuous and balanced life. By seeking out moderate pleasures and avoiding unnecessary pain, one could achieve a state of happiness that was both lasting and fulfilling.

Students interested in the philosophy of happiness may find Epicurus' teachings to be both insightful and practical. By focusing on cultivating inner peace, living in harmony with nature, and pursuing simple pleasures, one can achieve a state of happiness that is both sustainable and meaningful. By embracing the Epicurean concept of happiness, students can learn to appreciate the beauty of simplicity and find joy in the small moments of everyday life.

I.2.2 The pursuit of pleasure in Epicurean philosophy

In the pursuit of happiness, Epicurean philosophy offers a unique perspective on the role of pleasure. Epicurus, believed that the ultimate goal in life is to achieve a state of tranquility and contentment through the pursuit of pleasure. Unlike some other philosophical schools that equate pleasure with indulgence or hedonism, Epicurus argued that true pleasure comes from living a life of moderation and simplicity.

Epicurus distinguished between two types of pleasure: physical and mental. Physical pleasures, such as food and drink, are fleeting and ultimately unsatisfying. Mental pleasures, on the other hand, come from achieving a state of inner peace and contentment. According to Epicurus, the key to lasting happiness is to focus on cultivating mental pleasures rather than chasing after fleeting physical pleasures.

In Epicurean philosophy, the pursuit of pleasure is not about seeking out excessive or extravagant experiences. Instead, it is about finding joy and contentment in the simple pleasures of everyday life. Epicurus believed that true happiness comes from living a life of moderation and balance, free from unnecessary desires and distractions. By cultivating a sense of inner peace and contentment, individuals can experience a deeper and more lasting form of happiness.

One of the core principles of Epicurean philosophy is the ide a of ataraxia, or a state of tranquility and freedom from fear. By focusing on cultivating mental pleasures and avoiding unnecessary desires, individuals can achieve a sense of inner peace that leads to a more fulfilling and meaningful life. Epicurus believed that by living in harmony with nature and following the path of moderation, individuals can experience true happiness and contentment.

I.2.3 Overcoming fear and anxiety in Epicurean happiness

In the pursuit of happiness, it is common to face obstacles such as fear and anxiety that hinder our ability to experience true joy and contentment. However, in Epicurean philosophy, there are strategies that can help us overcome these negative emotions and achieve a sense of tranquility and peace.

One of the key teachings of Epicureanism is the belief that fear and anxiety are often rooted in irrational beliefs and can be conquered through rational thought and reflection. By examining the source of our fears and anxieties, we can identify the underlying causes and challenge them with reason and logic.

Another important aspect of overcoming fear and anxiety in Epicurean happiness is the practice of moderation and simplicity. By focusing on our basic needs and cultivating a sense of gratitude for the simple pleasures in life, we can reduce our reliance on material possessions and external sources of validation that often fuel our fears and anxieties.

Furthermore, Epicurean philosophy emphasizes the importance of cultivating meaningful relationships and connections with others as a way to combat fear and anxiety. By surrounding ourselves with positive and supportive individuals who share our values and beliefs, we can create a sense of community and belonging that helps us navigate life's challenges with greater ease and confidence.

Chapter II
Happiness in Eastern philosophy

Happiness takes on unique and profound meanings within Eastern philosophical traditions. Unlike the often individualistic and pleasure-driven view of happiness in Western thought, Eastern perspectives emphasize harmony, balance, and interconnectedness. These traditions frame happiness not as a fleeting emotional state but as a lasting condition of inner peace and alignment with the greater whole.

The philosophy encompasses a diverse array of traditions, including Hinduism, Tantra, Confucianism, Taoism, Buddhism, and others. While each offers unique insights and practices, several common themes run through these traditions, highlighting a shared understanding of the human condition and the path to fulfillment.

II.1 Happiness in Hinduism[1]

In Hinduism, the pursuit of happiness is deeply intertwined with spiritual growth, self-realization, and living in harmony with the cosmic order *(dharma)*. Happiness is not seen merely as a fleet-

---

[1] Hinduism is one of the oldest and most complex religions in the world, with a history stretching back over 4,000 years. It is more than just a religion; it is a way of life, encompassing a vast range of beliefs, practices, and cultural traditions.

ing emotion but as a profound state of inner peace, balance, and connection with the divine.

II.1.1 Four pursuits of life *(Purusharthas)*

Hindu philosophy outlines four primary goals for human life, known as the *Purusharthas:*

**Dharma* (righteousness and duty): Living in accordance with moral values and fulfilling one's responsibilities. Happiness arises from contributing to the greater good and aligning with the universe's natural order.

**Artha* (wealth and prosperity): The pursuit of material well-being is considered essential, but it must be balanced with ethics and social responsibility.

**Kama* (pleasure and desires): Enjoyment of sensory pleasures, relationships, and art is encouraged, as long as it does not violate dharma.

**Moksha* (liberation and self-realization): The ultimate goal is to attain liberation *(moksha),* transcending the cycle of birth and rebirth *(samsara).* This leads to eternal bliss and spiritual fulfillment.

II.1.2 Pathways to happiness *(yogas)*

Hinduism prescribes various spiritual disciplines *(yogas)* to achieve happiness:

**Bhakti yoga* (path of devotion): Devotional practices to connect with God. Through love and surrender, practitioners experience joy and divine grace.

**Karma yoga* (path of action): Selfless service without attachment to results brings inner peace and fulfillment.

**Jnana yoga* (path of knowledge): Seeking wisdom and self-inquiry lead to the realization of one's true nature *(Atman)* as blissful and eternal.

**Raja yoga* (path of meditation): Through meditation and mental discipline, one attains inner calm and bliss.

II.1.3 Detachment and contentment (v*airagya* and *santosha)*

* *Vairagya* (detachment): Recognizing the impermanent nature of worldly pleasures reduces suffering and fosters lasting peace.

* *Santosha* (contentment): Being satisfied with what one has and cultivating gratitude is a cornerstone of happiness.

II.1.4 The role of *dharma* and *karma*

Following one's *dharma* (duty) creates harmony, reducing internal conflict and fostering happiness.

* *Good karma* (right actions) leads to favorable outcomes in this life and future lives, contributing to happiness over time.

II.1.5 Celebration and festivals

Hindu culture is rich with festivals *(Diwali, Holi, Navaratri)* that celebrate life, joy, and togetherness, fostering communal happiness and reinforcing spiritual values.

II.1.6 Sacred texts and happiness

The ancient scriptures of India offer profound insights into the pursuit of happiness and fulfillment. The *Bhagavad Gita* (the second or first century BCE), teaches that true happiness lies in the sincere performance of one's duty, free from attachment to the fruits of action. By cultivating equanimity and dedicating actions to a higher purpose, one transcends fleeting emotions and experiences lasting peace.

The *Upanishads* (composed in Sanskrit between 800 and 400 BCE) delve deeper into the inner realm, emphasizing that genuine joy emerges from recognizing and realizing the divine essence within oneself. This realization dissolves the illusion of separateness, leading to a state of inner contentment and boundless bliss.

Complementing these philosophical works, the great epics—the *Ramayana* (ca 300 BCE) and the *Mahabbharata* (ca 3rd century BCE–4th century BCE)—illustrate through narrative how unwavering adherence to *dharma* (righteousness) creates harmony and prosperity in individual and societal life. Characters like Rama and Yudhishthira embody the principle that by aligning one's actions with dharma, even amidst trials, one finds enduring peace and fulfillment.

Together, these texts weave a holistic vision: happiness is not merely the result of external circumstances but a reflection of inner alignment with duty, truth, and the divine.

II.1.7 Balance between material and spiritual

Hinduism does not reject material pleasures but encourages a balanced life where spiritual growth and ethical conduct coexist with worldly pursuits.

Ultimately, Hinduism suggests that true and lasting happiness comes from within, through spiritual awakening and unity with the divine essence that permeates all existence.

II.2 Happiness in Tantra[2]

In Tantra, happiness is not seen as a fleeting emotion or mere pleasure but as a profound and sustained state of being—one that arises from inner alignment, spiritual realization, and the recognition of the divine within oneself and the universe. Tantra approaches happiness holistically, integrating body, mind, and spirit. It views all aspects of life, even the sensual and material, as potential pathways to transcendence and joy.

II.2.1 Happiness as union *(satchidananda)*

At the core of Tantra lies the idea of non-duality—the belief that the divine pervades everything. True happiness is found in the realization of oneness with the universe (Brahman or Shiva-Shakti). This state is referred to as *satchidananda* (existence, consciousness, bliss). Rather than seeking happiness externally, Tantra emphasizes the awakening of this innate bliss through spiritual practices.

---

[2] Tantra is a complex spiritual tradition that originated in India, influencing Hinduism, Buddhism, and Jainism. It involves rituals, meditation, mantras, and yogic practices aimed at expanding consciousness, achieving enlightenment, and integrating the physical with the spiritual.

II.2.2 Transmutation of desire

Tantra does not reject desire or sensory pleasure but seeks to transform and elevate it. By fully experiencing life with awareness, practitioners transcend ordinary pleasures and reach higher states of ecstasy. This is often symbolized by the merging of *shiva* (pure consciousness) and *shakti* (dynamic energy).

The goal is to savor life's experiences without attachment, finding joy in the fullness of the present moment.

II.2.3 Happiness through the body (embodied bliss)

Unlike ascetic paths that view the body as a hindrance, Tantra sees the body as a sacred vessel. Through practices like yoga, breathwork *(pranayama)*, and sacred sexuality, practitioners activate energy centers *(chakras)* to dissolve blockages and access higher states of joy.

* *Kundalini awakening*—the rising of dormant spiritual energy—is seen as a path to transcendental bliss.

II.2.4 The role of ritual and symbolism

Tantric rituals, mantras, and yantras serve to align the practitioner with cosmic forces. Rituals are not performed for external rewards but to internalize divine qualities. This generates a profound sense of connection and inner happiness.

II.2.5 The concept of *lila* (divine play)

Tantra views existence as *lila,* the cosmic play of the divine. Recognizing life as a dance of opposites—joy and sorrow, light and dark—fosters an attitude of detachment and acceptance. This playful perspective on life reduces suffering and amplifies happiness by encouraging the practitioner to flow with the rhythms of life.

II.2.6 Integration of shadow and light

Tantra acknowledges the shadow—our fears, desires, and suppressed emotions. By embracing and integrating these aspects, practitioners dissolve inner conflicts, leading to a more authentic and sustained happiness.

* *Kundalini awakening*—the rising of dormant spiritual energy—is seen as a path to transcendental bliss.

Happiness emerges not by rejecting darkness but by illuminating it with awareness.

II.2.7 Practical approaches to cultivate happiness in Tantra

* *Meditation (Dhyana)* – Cultivates inner peace and clarity.

* *Visualization (Bhavana)* – Engages the imagination to manifest joy and bliss.

* *Mantra (sacred sound)* – Elevates consciousness through vibrational alignment.

* *Service and compassion* – Recognizes the divine in others, fostering interconnected happiness.

* *Sexual alchemy* – Uses intimacy as a path to divine connection. Its concept blends mysticism, spirituality, and sexuality, often drawing from ancient esoteric traditions like Taoism, Tantra, Hermeticism,[3] and Western occultism.[4] It views sexual energy not just

---

[3] Hermeticism, also known as Hermetism, is a spiritual, philosophical, and esoteric tradition based primarily on writings attributed to Hermes Trismegistus, a

as a source of pleasure or procreation but as a powerful force for spiritual transformation, enlightenment, and personal empowerment.

The essence of sexual alchemy lies in the ability to transform raw sexual energy (often called *libido* or life force) into higher spiritual states. This mirrors the broader alchemical principle of turning "base metals into gold," where sexual energy (the "base") is refined into spiritual enlightenment (the "gold").

Sexual alchemy emphasizes the merging of dualities—masculine and feminine energies (sometimes referred to as *Shiva* and *Shakti* in Tantra or the Solar and Lunar principles in Hermeticism). This union can occur within an individual (inner alchemy) or between partners (outer alchemy).

Practitioners use sexual practices to awaken dormant spiritual energies, such as *Kundalini* in Tantra. This energy rises through the body's energy centers *(chakras),* leading to expanded consciousness and enlightenment.

Sexual acts can be part of sacred rituals, often seen as a reenactment of cosmic creation myths. In this sense, sexual union is a microcosm of the divine creative process, with the body serving as the "temple."

---

legendary Hellenistic figure associated with the Egyptian god Thoth and the Greek god Hermes. The tradition emerged in late antiquity and profoundly influenced the Renaissance and Western esoteric movements.

[4] Western occultism encompasses a broad range of esoteric and mystical traditions that have evolved over centuries in Europe and the Western world. It blends ancient philosophies, religious practices, mysticism, and symbolic systems.

Sexual alchemy distinguishes between ordinary, desire-driven sex and sex performed with awareness, intention, and reverence. The latter is seen as a spiritual practice that elevates the soul.

II.3 Happiness in Confucianism[5]

In Confucianism, happiness is not understood as mere personal pleasure or fleeting joy. Instead, it is deeply rooted in the cultivation of virtue, harmonious relationships, and the fulfillment of social roles. The Confucian path to happiness emphasizes moral development, social harmony, and a life of meaning and responsibility.

II.3.1 Moral virtue and self-cultivation

Confucius believed that happiness arises from the cultivation of moral character. The process of becoming a virtuous person—through the practice of *ren* (benevolence), *li* (ritual propriety), *yi* (righteousness), and *zhi* (wisdom)—leads to inner peace and joy. For Confucius, self-cultivation is not an isolated pursuit but a lifelong engagement in refining one's behavior and aligning it with moral principles.

II.3.2 Harmony in relationships

[5] Confucianism is an ancient Chinese philosophical and ethical system founded by Confucius (Kong Fuzi, 551–479 BCE). It emphasizes moral integrity, social harmony, and the importance of proper relationships. Over the centuries, Confucianism evolved into a comprehensive worldview that shaped East Asian cultures, influencing governance, education, family structure, and personal conduct.

Happiness in Confucianism is deeply connected to one's relationships with others. The Five Relationships (between ruler and subject, parent and child, husband and wife, elder and younger sibling, and friend and friend) serve as a foundation for social stability and personal fulfillment. By fulfilling one's role in these relationships with sincerity and respect, individuals contribute to societal harmony, which is seen as a source of collective well-being and personal happiness.

II.3.3 Social responsibility and service

A key aspect of happiness is the sense of purpose derived from serving others and contributing to the greater good. Confucius taught that individuals are happiest when they act in accordance with the needs of society, family, and community. This reflects the Confucian belief that personal fulfillment cannot be separated from social obligations.

II.3.4 Balance and moderation

Confucius advocated for a balanced life guided by the principle of *zhongyong* (the doctrine of the mean). This idea encourages moderation, avoiding extremes, and finding harmony between personal desires and social expectations. Such balance fosters stability, which is essential for enduring happiness.

II.3.5 Learning and wisdom

The pursuit of knowledge and reflection is another pathway to happiness. Confucius saw learning not just as an intellectual exercise but as a way to better oneself and understand the world. A person who continuously learns and applies wisdom is more likely to experience fulfillment and joy.

II.3.6 Happiness as a byproduct, not a goal

In Confucianism, happiness is not sought directly but emerges naturally as a byproduct of living a virtuous and meaningful life. This perspective contrasts with hedonistic views, suggesting that true happiness lies in selflessness, moral integrity, and the pursuit of collective harmony.

II.3.7 The role of ritual and tradition

Li (ritual) plays a crucial role in fostering happiness by instilling a sense of order, beauty, and connection with others. Through rituals, individuals cultivate discipline and express reverence for their ancestors and society, reinforcing their place in the larger social fabric.

II.3.8 Modern implications

In contemporary society, Confucian ideals of happiness continue to resonate, particularly in East Asian cultures where community, family values, and education are prioritized. The Confucian model offers an alternative to individualistic notions of happiness, emphasizing that well-being arises from ethical living, social harmony, and the pursuit of collective good.

II.4 Happiness in Daoism[6]

Daoism means "non-action" or effortless action. This doesn't imply laziness but rather flowing with life naturally and responding to situations intuitively. For Daoists, forcing outcomes creates stress and disharmony, while allowing things to unfold organically leads to greater contentment and well-being.

Example: A river flowing around rocks symbolizes *wu wei.* By adapting to obstacles instead of fighting against them, the river continues its course – just as a person should align with life's rhythms.

II.4.1 Harmony with nature

Daoists believe that nature embodies the Dao perfectly. Observing and emulating the natural world can foster happiness. Simplicity and a return to nature reflect a rejection of excessive desires or artificial constructs that lead to dissatisfaction.

Practice: Spending time in nature, gardening, or meditating outdoors are ways Daoists cultivate happiness by attuning themselves to the natural world.

II.4.2 Simplicity *(Pu,* the uncarved block)

[6] Daoism (or Taoism) is traditionally attributed to Laozi (Lao Tzu), who is believed to have lived in the 6th century BCE, but the *Tao Te Ching* (the foundational text) was likely written between the 4th and 3rd centuries BCE. This ancient Chinese philosophical and spiritual tradition emphasizes living in harmony with the *Dao (Tao),* which translates to "The Way" or "The Path." It is both a philosophy and a religion, influencing Chinese culture for over two millennia.

Happiness arises from simplicity and humility. The Daoist concept of *pu* (the uncarved block) suggests that one should remain in a pure, unadulterated state, free from excessive refinement or complexity. Simplicity allows for clarity and genuine joy without the burdens of unnecessary desires.

* *Living simply:* Reducing material possessions, avoiding overcomplication, and appreciating the present moment contribute to lasting happiness.

II.4.3 Acceptance and flexibility

A key source of happiness in Daoism is accepting life as it is, rather than resisting change or clinging to rigid expectations. Daoists view the world as constantly evolving, and by remaining flexible and open-minded, individuals experience greater inner peace.

Parable of the Farmer

A well-known Daoist story tells of a farmer who loses his horse. His neighbors lament the bad luck, but the farmer simply responds, *"Who knows if it is good or bad?"* When the horse returns with a group of wild horses, the neighbors celebrate his fortune, but again, he replies the same. This parable highlights how happiness comes from detachment from rigid judgments of events.

II.4.4 Inner alchemy and self-cultivation

Daoist practices like Tai Chi, Qigong, and meditation are aimed at cultivating *qi* (life force energy) and harmonizing mind, body, and spirit. This cultivation leads to a deeper, more stable form of happiness that is not dependent on external circumstances.

Result: Through self-awareness and self-cultivation, Daoists achieve inner tranquility and joy.

II.4.5 Embracing paradox and mystery

Daoism acknowledges the paradoxical nature of life – that happiness and sorrow are intertwined. By embracing both light and dark, success and failure, individuals avoid becoming overly attached to fleeting emotions and experience a more balanced, sustained happiness.

II.5 Happiness in Buddhism[7]

The Buddhist concept of happiness is deeply rooted in the philosophy of inner peace, detachment, and the cessation of suffering. Unlike Western notions that often link happiness to external achievements or sensory pleasures, Buddhism emphasizes an inward journey toward enlightenment and liberation *(nirvana).*

II.5.1 Happiness as the absence of suffering *(dukkha)*

Buddhism teaches that suffering *(dukkha)* is an inherent part of life. The Buddha's First Noble Truth acknowledges this universal suffering. However, happiness is not the pursuit of fleeting pleasures but the gradual diminishing of suffering through wisdom, ethical conduct, and mental discipline.

---

[7] Buddhism is a spiritual tradition and philosophical system that originated in India around the 5th to 4th century BCE. It is based on the teachings of Siddhartha Gautama, known as the Buddha, who attained enlightenment and dedicated his life to teaching others the path to liberation from suffering.

"Happiness does not depend on what you have or who you are. It solely relies on what you think."

II.5.2 The path to happiness – The noble eightfold path

Buddhism provides a structured path to achieve happiness through the Noble Eightfold Path, which consists of:

1. Right view (understanding the nature of suffering)
2. Right intention (commitment to ethical and compassionate living)
3. Right speech
4. Right action
5. Right livelihood
6. Right effort
7. Right mindfulness
8. Right concentration

By following this path, individuals cultivate a peaceful mind and experience contentment that arises from ethical living and self-awareness.

II.5.3 The role of detachment (non-clinging)

Buddhism teaches that attachment to material goods, relationships, and even personal identity is a major source of suffering. Happiness emerges when one lets go of these attachments and lives with non-attachment *(upekkha)*.

This does not mean rejecting life but engaging with it without craving or aversion.

Example:

A lotus flower grows in muddy water but remains unstained. Similarly, happiness in Buddhism thrives in detachment and equanimity.

II.5.4 Loving-kindness and compassion *(metta* and *karuna)*

Buddhist happiness extends beyond the self. True happiness arises from cultivating love *(metta)* and compassion *(karuna)* for others. By alleviating the suffering of others, one indirectly fosters inner peace and joy.

Practice:

**Metta bhavana* (loving-kindness meditation) generates feelings of goodwill for oneself and others, leading to a profound sense of connection and fulfillment.

II.5.5 Mindfulness and present moment awareness

Happiness is found in the present moment, not in regrets of the past or anxieties about the future. Mindfulness *(sati)* anchors individuals in the here and now, allowing them to appreciate life as it unfolds.

"There is no path to happiness; happiness is the path."

II.5.6 The ultimate happiness – *Nirvana*

Nirvana represents the ultimate state of happiness in Buddhism, characterized by the cessation of all suffering and the liberation from the cycle of birth, death, and rebirth *(samsara)*. This transcendent state is marked by profound peace and unshakable serenity.

Key idea:

While *nirvana* may seem distant, even small steps toward inner peace through meditation and ethical conduct can bring glimpses of this happiness into daily life.

II.5.7 Practical applications for daily life

* *Gratitude and simplicity:* Practicing gratitude and living simply can lead to happiness by reducing desires and fostering contentment.

* *Service to others:* Volunteering, offering kindness, and engaging in acts of compassion promote a sense of fulfillment.

* *Meditation:* Regular meditation calms the mind and fosters a deep sense of peace.

II.5.8 Zen and happiness in the present

Zen Buddhism, a branch of Mahayana Buddhism, emphasizes direct experience and mindfulness in the present moment. Zen practitioners seek happiness not in the future but in the simplicity of everyday life. Practices such as meditation *(zazen)* cultivate awareness, stripping away mental clutter and fostering a sense of profound contentment.

In summary, the Buddhist approach to happiness is holistic, emphasizing the cultivation of inner peace, ethical living, and a compassionate heart. It suggests that true and lasting happiness arises not from external circumstances but from the mind's capacity to remain peaceful and free from attachments.

II.6 Common and different threads among the different Eastern philosophies

Common threads

* *Interconnectedness:* A prevailing theme in Eastern thought is the interconnectedness of all things. Whether expressed through the Buddhist concept of dependent origination, the Taoist notion of living in harmony with the Tao, or the Hindu understanding of Brahman as the ultimate reality, there is a recognition that personal well-being is intrinsically linked to the well-being of others and the universe. Compassion, empathy, and altruism naturally arise from this awareness.

* *Impermanence:* Eastern traditions emphasize the transient nature of life. In Buddhism, the concept of impermanence *(anicca)* teaches that all phenomena are subject to change, leading practitioners to cultivate detachment and presence. Taoism similarly acknowledges the ever-shifting flow of existence, advocating for adaptability and acceptance. This understanding fosters a deeper appreciation for the present moment and reduces attachment to fleeting desires and possessions.

* *Inner Peace:* Happiness and fulfillment in Eastern philosophy are seen as internal states, not dependent on external circumstances. Practices such as meditation, mindfulness, and ethical living cultivate inner tranquility. Confucianism emphasizes cultivating virtue and harmonious relationships, while Taoism advocates simplicity and alignment with the natural order. This inward focus contrasts with more external, goal-oriented approaches to happiness.

Different threads

* *Path to enlightenment:* While interconnectedness and inner peace are common, the methods to achieve them differ. Buddhism advocates the Noble Eightfold Path, emphasizing ethical conduct, mental discipline, and wisdom. Taoism, on the other hand, promotes effortless action *(wu wei)* and following the flow of nature. Hinduism offers a multiplicity of paths *(yogas)* suited to different temperaments, including devotion *(bhakti),* knowledge *(jnana),* and selfless action *(karma).*

* *Role of the self:* In Buddhism, the self is seen as an illusion, with liberation arising from transcending ego and attachment. Hinduism, however, views the self *(atman)* as ultimately one with Brahman, suggesting a unity between individual and cosmic consciousness. Confucianism focuses more on the self as a relational being, whose development occurs through social harmony and ethical responsibilities.

* *Engagement with the world:* Confucianism places great importance on societal roles, family, and governance, advocating active engagement with the world to cultivate virtue and harmony. Taoism often takes a more reclusive or passive stance, suggesting that true wisdom lies in non-interference and living in accordance with nature. Buddhism navigates between these extremes, encouraging compassion and engagement while recognizing the ultimate goal of transcending worldly attachments.

Chapter III
Happiness in Islamic philosophy[8]

Islamic philosophy occupies a unique position that bridges both Eastern and Western traditions. Categorizing it strictly as one or the other is not entirely accurate, as its development reflects influences from a variety of intellectual traditions and geographical contexts.

Rather than fitting neatly into either Eastern or Western philosophy, Islamic philosophy can be seen as a synthesis that transcends the dichotomy between Eastern and Western thought.

III.1 Happiness in the works of Arabic and Islamic philosophers

---

[8] Islamic philosophy originated in the Middle East, North Africa, and parts of Asia, regions traditionally associated with Eastern thought. It shares historical and cultural ties with other Eastern traditions, such as Indian and Persian philosophies. It often incorporates mystical elements, such as in Sufism, which resonates with other Eastern mystical traditions like Taoism. However, Islamic philosophy's emphasis on reason and logic aligns with the methodologies of Western philosophy. Through translations and commentaries, Islamic philosophy became a crucial link in transmitting Greek ideas to medieval Europe, influencing Western thought.

Happiness has been a central theme in the works of Arabic and Islamic philosophers, particularly during the Islamic Golden Age (8th to 14th centuries). Philosophers such as Al-Farabi, Ibn Sina (Avicenna), and Al-Ghazali explored happiness from various perspectives, blending Aristotelian and Neoplatonic ideas with Islamic philosophy and theology.

III.1.1 Al-Farabi (872–950 CE): The virtuous city

Al-Farabi, often referred to as "The Second Teacher" (with Aristotle being the first), occupies a central place in medieval Islamic philosophy. His works reflect a synthesis of Platonic, Aristotelian, and Neoplatonic ideas, adapted to the intellectual and cultural context of the Islamic world. Al-Farabi believed that the highest purpose of human life is the attainment of ultimate happiness. For him, philosophy and rational inquiry serve as the essential means to reach this goal, elevating the soul beyond the material realm to grasp universal truths.

III.1.1.1 The role of reason

Central to Al-Farabi's philosophy is the concept of reason *(ʿaql)*. He viewed reason as the defining characteristic of human beings, enabling them to comprehend the natural order and the divine. In his view, the rational soul must cultivate virtues and align itself with higher intellectual and spiritual realities to achieve happiness. This process involves constant self-reflection, education, and the pursuit of knowledge, leading to the perfection of the intellect.

III.1.1.2 The Virtuous City

One of Al-Farabi's most influential contributions is his political philosophy, particularly his vision of the Virtuous City. In this ideal society, governance is entrusted to a philosopher-king whose wisdom mirrors that of the divine. Al-Farabi argued that just as the rational soul governs the body, a wise ruler must guide society towards collective happiness and moral excellence. The well-being of individuals, he asserted, is inseparable from the prosperity of the community.

The virtuous city is structured hierarchically, with each class contributing to the greater good according to its capacity. Al-Farabi contrasted this ideal with ignorant, immoral, and straying cities, which he believed failed to cultivate virtue and instead promoted materialism and discord.

III.1.1.3 Eternal happiness

Al-Farabi distinguished between two forms of happiness: worldly and eternal. While worldly happiness is transient and tied to physical pleasures or societal success, eternal happiness is enduring and rooted in intellectual and spiritual enlightenment. Achieving eternal happiness requires transcending the material world and attaining unity with the Active Intellect *(al-^{c}aql al-fa^{cc}āl)*, a concept Al-Farabi borrowed from Aristotle and further developed within his metaphysical framework.

In this framework, the philosopher emerges as the ideal model of human perfection, having realized the fullest potential of reason and achieved harmony with universal truths. This vision not only reinforces the value of philosophical inquiry but also underscores the transformative power of knowledge in shaping both individuals and society.

III.1.2 Ibn Sina (980-1037 CE): Bridging Aristotelian philosophy and Islamic thought

Ibn Sina, also known in the Latin West as Avicenna, stood at the intersection of Greek philosophical heritage—primarily Aristotelian and Neo-Platonic ideas—and the Islamic theological tradition. He sought to harmonize reason with revelation, proposing that truth could be approached via rational inquiry, yet remained firmly grounded in the reality of divine creation and the soul's immortality.

III.1.2.1 The soul's fulfillment as the essence of happiness

Central to Ibn Sina's account of happiness is the conviction that each human being is endowed with a rational soul capable of ascending to higher levels of understanding. For him, "happiness" is not merely a fleeting emotion but the actualization of the soul's inherent potential. In other words, the soul realizes its ultimate purpose—and, thus, happiness—when it perfects its intellectual capacities and aligns itself with the divine source.

III.1.2.2 Hierarchy of joy

Ibn Sina describes a gradation of happiness or joy, each level corresponding to a different aspect of human life: physical, moral, intellectual/spiritual, and ultimately, eschatological (pertaining to the afterlife). While each level provides its own kind of pleasure or contentment, only the highest forms yield lasting fulfillment.

III.1.2.3 Physical pleasures: Basic and temporary

At the lowest level, Ibn Sina recognizes the innate human inclination toward bodily or sensory pleasures—such as satisfying hunger, thirst, and other appetites. While these pleasures are real and natural, they are by their nature fleeting and incapable of providing enduring contentment.

* *Reason's role:* Even here, reason can guide physical desires so that they serve healthy ends rather than become enslaving or destructive.

* *Limitations:* Since these pleasures fade quickly and often leave a sense of longing behind, they cannot represent the soul's true and ultimate happiness.

III.1.2.4 Moral happiness: virtuous actions and ethical living

A step above physical satisfaction lies moral or ethical happiness. This level involves aligning one's actions with virtue and justice.

* *Cultivation of virtues:* By cultivating virtues such as temperance, courage, and generosity, a person experiences inner satisfaction and a well-ordered life.

* *Social harmony:* Ethical living also ensures harmony within one's community, illustrating the importance of moral conduct not just for the individual but for society.

* *Higher than physical pleasures:* Though moral happiness is more stable than bodily pleasures, Ibn Sina still sees it as a preparatory stage for something even deeper—namely, intellectual and spiritual fulfillment.

III.1.2.5 Intellectual and spiritual bliss: Unity with the Active Intellect

For Ibn Sina, the highest level achievable in earthly life is intellectual and spiritual happiness, which he describes as the contemplation of divine realities and union with the "Active Intellect."

* *The Active Intellect:* A concept adapted from Neo-Platonic and Aristotelian thought, the Active Intellect is an intermediary between the human mind and the divine realm. Through rigorous philosophical inquiry and spiritual discipline, the human intellect can bridge the gap between the material and immaterial realms.

* *Contemplation and understanding:* As one refines their rational faculty—studying metaphysics, reflecting on divine attributes, and engaging in philosophical contemplation—their intellect draws closer to the universal truths that emanate from the divine.

* *Spiritual dimension:* This intellectual ascent is simultaneously spiritual, as the soul purifies itself and harmonizes with eternal verities. When the mind contemplates the highest truths, the soul experiences deep, abiding joy that far surpasses mundane pleasures.

III.1.2.6 The Afterlife: Eternal connection with the Divine Essence

While intellectual and spiritual happiness can be approached in this life, Ibn Sina posits that the soul reaches its fullest, most perfect joy after death, when it is no longer restricted by the limitations of the body.

* *Immortality of the soul:* Drawing on philosophical arguments for the soul's immaterial and imperishable nature, Ibn Sina holds that the rational soul survives the body's dissolution.

* *Eschatological fulfillment:* In the afterlife, the soul achieves a direct, unmediated connection with the divine essence (or with ultimate truth). This culminates in a perfect state of happiness beyond any earthly experience.

* *Alignment with Islamic theology:* Ibn Sina's view resonates with key Islamic beliefs regarding the soul's immortality and final return to God, yet retains a distinctly philosophical framework explaining how such ultimate fulfillment is possible.

III.1.2.7 Practical implications and legacy

According to Ibn Sina, genuine happiness requires a deliberate effort to cultivate one's intellect and moral virtues. He encouraged systematic study of the sciences (both physical and metaphysical), along with a disciplined ethical life. Such a holistic approach integrates body, soul, and mind in a unified quest for fulfillment.

III.1.2.8 Influence on later thinkers

Ibn Sina's hierarchical approach to happiness influenced both Islamic and Western medieval philosophers. Scholastics like Thomas Aquinas grappled with Avicenna's arguments, integrating and modifying them within a Christian context. Within the Islamic tradition, Ibn Sina paved the way for subsequent thinkers—such as

Suhrawardi, Mulla Sadra, and others—to investigate the soul's journey toward perfection.

III.1.2.9 Relevance today

Even in modern discussions of well-being and human fulfillment, Ibn Sina's emphasis on integrating ethical living, intellectual development, and spiritual insight remains resonant. His approach reminds us that while material comfort and ethical structures are vital, the deepest sense of happiness may lie in continually refining our understanding of reality and cultivating a spiritual awareness of what transcends our everyday experience.

III.1.3 Al-Ghazali (1058–1111 CE): Reconciliation of religion and philosophy

III.1.3.1 Critique of philosophers

Al-Ghazali's intellectual journey led him to confront the prevailing philosophical traditions of his time, particularly those of Al-Farabi and Ibn Sina. In his seminal work *The Incoherence of the Philosophers (Tahāfut al-falāsifa),* Al-Ghazali presented a rigorous critique of these philosophers, accusing them of over-relying on reason while diminishing the role of divine revelation. He contended that although philosophy offers valuable insights into the natural world, it falls short when addressing metaphysical truths and the ultimate purpose of human existence. Al-Ghazali believed that certain philosophical claims contradicted Islamic teachings, especially regarding the nature of God, the soul, and the afterlife. His critique was not a blanket rejection of philosophy but a call to prioritize religious knowledge as the highest form of wisdom.

III.1.3.2 Happiness in religion

For Al-Ghazali, true happiness is inseparable from faith and devotion to God. He argued that the pursuit of happiness must align with the comprehensive teachings of Islam, which encompass spiritual, moral, and intellectual dimensions. In works like *The Revival of the Religious Sciences* ***(Iḥyā' ᶜulum al-dīn),*** Al-Ghazali outlined how acts of worship, ethical conduct, and the pursuit of knowledge foster inner peace and contentment. Unlike philosophers who placed intellectual enlightenment as the pinnacle of happiness, Al-Ghazali maintained that happiness is ultimately a byproduct of submission to God's will and adherence to Islamic principles.

III.1.3.3 The heart's purification

A cornerstone of Al-Ghazali's thought is the concept of the purification of the heart. He emphasized that achieving happiness requires self-discipline, moral refinement, and detachment from materialistic desires. Al-Ghazali taught that the heart, if left unchecked, can become clouded by greed, pride, and other spiritual ailments. Through practices such as prayer, fasting, and remembrance of God, individuals can cleanse their hearts and draw closer to divine presence. This inward journey, according to Al-Ghazali, not only brings about personal tranquility but also harmonizes the soul with the higher realities of existence.

III.1.3.4 The Hereafter

Al-Ghazali's understanding of happiness extends beyond the temporal world, centering on the concept of eternal bliss in the hereafter. He posited that ultimate happiness is achieved through proximity to God in the afterlife. This vision stands in contrast to philosophical traditions that emphasized worldly fulfillment or intellectual satisfaction. Al-Ghazali taught that the soul's journey continues after death, and the quality of one's actions and faith in this life determines their state in the next. As such, he encouraged believers to live with the awareness that their pursuit of happiness is intricately linked to their spiritual growth and relationship with God.

III.1.4 Ibn Rushd (Averroes) (1126–1198 CE): Rationalism and happiness

Ibn Rushd, also known as Averroes, stands as one of the most influential figures in the intersection of philosophy and religion. His defense of reason and rational inquiry set him apart as a key thinker in medieval Islamic and Western thought.

III.1.4.1 Defending reason

Ibn Rushd argued that philosophy and religion are not contradictory but rather complementary paths to achieving happiness and truth. He maintained that both serve to illuminate the same reality, albeit through different approaches. For Ibn Rushd, philosophical investigation leads to a deeper understanding of the divine, while religious faith provides a moral framework accessible to the broader population. This harmonization of reason and faith was essential to his vision of a just and enlightened society.

III.1.4.2 The Active Intellect

Building on the works of previous philosophers like Ibn Sina, Ibn Rushd emphasized the role of the Active Intellect in the pursuit of knowledge and happiness. The Active Intellect, according to Ibn Rushd, acts as the bridge between the human mind and universal truths. Through the cultivation of intellectual virtues and engagement with philosophical inquiry, individuals can attain the highest form of enlightenment. This process leads not only to personal fulfillment but also to a greater understanding of the cosmos and one's place within it.

III.1.4.3 Practical ethics

Beyond metaphysical and epistemological pursuits, Ibn Rushd placed significant importance on ethical conduct and rational decision-making in daily life. He believed that the practice of virtue and adherence to rational principles were fundamental to individual and collective well-being. By promoting ethical behavior and critical thinking, Ibn Rushd sought to create a society where happiness could be achieved through justice, cooperation, and intellectual development.

III.2 Happiness in Sufism[9]

In Sufism, a mystical and spiritual dimension of Islam, happiness is not merely an emotional or psychological state but a profound and spiritual condition tied to the soul's journey toward unity with the Divine. Unlike fleeting worldly pleasures, Sufi happiness is rooted in inner peace, self-awareness, and divine love. This concept of happiness transcends materialism, focusing instead on spiritual fulfillment and the realization of higher truths.

III.2.1 Divine proximity and union

In Sufism, the ultimate source of happiness is nearness to God (Allah). The Sufi seeks to dissolve the ego *(nafs)* and achieve annihilation in God ***(fanā')***. This self-transcendence allows the seeker to experience the eternal bliss of divine presence. In this state, worldly troubles become insignificant, as the heart is content with God's remembrance *(dhikr)* and immersed in divine love ***(ʿishq)***.

"When the soul is in union with the Divine, it tastes a joy that is incomparable to any earthly happiness."

III.2.2 Contentment and acceptance

A hallmark of Sufi happiness is contentment with God's decree. By practicing one's acceptance of fate and surrendering to the divine will, Sufis cultivate an inner peace that shields them from the disturbances of life's hardships. This leads to a deep, unwavering

---

[9] Sufism focuses on inner purification, love, and the pursuit of divine closeness. Rooted in the teachings of the Qur'an and Hadith, Sufism emphasizes the esoteric aspects of Islam, promoting a personal and experiential connection with God.

form of happiness rooted in trust (tawakkul) in God's wisdom and mercy.

Rumi says:

"When the soul lies down in that grass, the world is too full to talk about. Ideas, language—even the phrase each other—doesn't make any sense."

III.2.3 Love and ecstasy

Sufis often describe happiness as an ecstatic state achieved through divine love. This love burns away the self and fills the heart with light and joy. The heart, intoxicated by love *(sukr),* transcends the material world and finds joy in the simplest divine experiences. Sufi poets like Rumi, Hafez, and Ibn Arabi speak of this love as the primary gateway to true happiness.

"With life's pains, a hidden joy flows beneath; for the heart that loves sees the Beloved in all things."

III.2.4 The role of *dhikr* (Remembrance of God)

Dhikr, the continuous remembrance of God, is central to cultivating happiness in Sufism. The repetition of divine names purifies the heart, calming the restless mind and aligning the soul with divine harmony. This practice lifts the soul to a plane of spiritual joy, making the seeker feel connected and content.

"Verily, in the remembrance of God do hearts find rest." – Qur'an (13:28)

III.2.5 Serving others

Happiness in Sufism is not a solitary pursuit but is often found in serving others. By selflessly aiding creation, the Sufi reflects divine mercy and experiences joy in seeing the reflection of God in those they help. This service brings a sense of purpose and fulfillment.

III.2.6 The paradox of pain and joy

Sufism teaches that pain and suffering are often necessary paths to spiritual growth. Through trials, the ego is broken, allowing divine light to penetrate. Hence, happiness is not the absence of suffering but the ability to find joy and meaning within it.

"*The wound is the place where the Light enters you.*" – Rumi

III.3 Key themes across philosophers

* *Dual nature of happiness:* Most Arabic philosophers distinguished between worldly and eternal happiness, with a consensus that the latter is superior.

* *Intellectual and spiritual fulfillment:* Happiness involves developing the intellect and aligning the soul with divine principles.

* *Ethical conduct:* Virtuous behavior and moral living are indispensable for achieving happiness.

* *Integration of philosophy and religion:* While approaches varied, there was an overarching attempt to reconcile philosophical reasoning with Islamic teachings.

Arabic philosophers thus presented a nuanced understanding of happiness, blending reason, ethics, and spirituality. Their ideas continue to influence discussions on happiness and well-being in both Eastern and Western thoughts.

Chapter IV
Happiness in contemporary philosophy

The concept of happiness in contemporary philosophy is multifaceted, engaging with ideas from ethics, psychology, political philosophy, and existential thought. Unlike classical approaches that often tied happiness to virtue (Aristotle) or pleasure (Epicurus), contemporary philosophers explore happiness through subjective experiences, well-being, and the structure of human life in a complex, often unpredictable world.

IV.1 Subjective vs. objective well-being

Contemporary discussions often distinguish between subjective happiness (personal satisfaction and positive emotions) and objective well-being (measurable life quality, health, and flourishing). Philosophers like Martha Nussbaum and Amartya Sen advocate for the "capabilities approach," which sees happiness as dependent on an individual's ability to achieve valuable life goals.

IV.2 Psychological insights and positive psychology

Positive psychology is a relatively new field that focuses on the study of positive emotions, strengths, and virtues that contribute to well-being and happiness. Unlike traditional approaches that focus on the absence of negative emotions or problems, positive psychology looks at what makes life worth living and how individuals can thrive and flourish. This approach emphasizes the importance of positive experiences, relationships, and personal growth in achieving happiness.

Philosophers increasingly draw on findings from positive psychology (e.g., Martin Seligman's work on flourishing and Mihaly Csikszentmihalyi's concept of flow). This interdisciplinary approach treats happiness not as mere pleasure but as a state of engagement and meaning.

One of the key principles of positive psychology is the idea that happiness is not just the absence of sadness or distress, but a state of overall well-being and fulfillment. This perspective aligns closely with the teachings of Stoic and Epicurean philosophy, which also emphasize the importance of cultivating inner virtues and living a life of virtue and moderation. Positive psychology encourages individuals to focus on their strengths and values, rather than being consumed by negative thoughts or emotions.

Positive psychology also draws on the insights of environmental ethics, which emphasizes the interconnectedness between humans and the natural world. This perspective recognizes that our environment plays a crucial role in shaping our well-being and happiness, and advocates for sustainable practices that promote the health and happiness of both individuals and the planet. By fostering a sense of connection to nature and promoting environmental stewardship, positive psychology seeks to enhance our overall sense of well-being and happiness.

One key aspect of positive psychology is the emphasis on positive emotions and experiences. Research has shown that cultivating positive emotions such as gratitude, kindness, and love can lead to greater happiness and life satisfaction. By focusing on what brings us joy and fulfillment, we can enhance our overall well-being and sense of purpose. This highlights the importance of engaging in activities that bring us pleasure and meaning, as these experiences can have a lasting impact on our happiness.

Another important aspect is the concept of resilience. Resilience refers to our ability to bounce back from adversity and overcome challenges. By developing resilience, we can better navigate life's ups and downs and maintain a positive outlook even in difficult times. This resilience can help us build a strong foundation for happiness and well-being, as it allows us to adapt to change and grow from our experiences.

Positive psychology also emphasizes the importance of social connections and relationships in promoting happiness. Research has shown that strong social connections are a key predictor of happiness and life satisfaction. By nurturing our relationships with family, friends, and community, we can strengthen our support network and enhance our overall well-being. This highlights the value of fostering meaningful connections with others and prioritizing our social interactions as a way to cultivate happiness.

IV.3 Environmental ethics

The environment plays a crucial role in shaping human happiness. From the air we breathe to the natural landscapes that surround us, our surroundings have a profound impact on our well-being. In the field of philosophy of happiness, scholars have long debated the significance of environmental factors in determining our overall happiness. Some argue that a connection to nature is essential for human flourishing, while others believe that our inner attitudes are more important than external circumstances.

In the realm of positive psychology, researchers have studied the impact of environmental factors on human happiness and well-being. Studies have shown that exposure to natural environments can reduce stress, improve mood, and enhance overall mental health. Positive psychologists emphasize the importance of engaging with nature and creating environments that support positive emotions and personal growth. By fostering connections to the natural world, individuals can enhance their sense of happiness and fulfillment.

Environmental ethics also play a crucial role in shaping human happiness. Ethical considerations such as sustainability, conservation, and respect for the natural world are essential for promoting a harmonious relationship between humans and the environment. By adopting ethical practices that prioritize the well-being of all living beings and the preservation of the planet, individuals can contribute to a more sustainable and fulfilling future for themselves and future generations. Ultimately, the impact of the environment on human happiness is a complex and multifaceted issue that requires a holistic approach to understanding and addressing.

One key ethical consideration in environmental happiness is the idea of sustainability. In order to achieve true happiness, we must ensure that our actions are sustainable and do not harm the environment in the long term. This means being mindful of our consumption habits, reducing waste, and supporting eco-friendly practices. By living in harmony with the natural world, we can cultivate a sense of connection and fulfillment that goes beyond material possessions.

Another important ethical consideration is the idea of interdependence. As students of philosophy, we understand that everything in the universe is connected in some way. This means that our actions have ripple effects that can impact not only ourselves but also other living beings and the environment as a whole. By recognizing our interconnectedness with all of existence, we can cultivate a sense of empathy and compassion that can lead to greater happiness and well-being for ourselves and others.

Furthermore, ethical considerations in environmental happiness also involve the concept of stewardship. As stewards of the Earth, it is our responsibility to protect and preserve the natural world for future generations. This means taking proactive measures to address issues such as climate change, pollution, and habitat destruction. By acting as responsible caretakers of the planet, we can contribute to a more sustainable and harmonious world that fosters happiness and well-being for all beings.

IV.4 Hedonism and life satisfaction

Hedonistic theories continue to influence happiness studies, arguing that happiness arises from pleasure and the absence of pain. However, thinkers like Fred Feldman refine this by proposing that happiness consists of attitudinal pleasures over time, rather than just momentary joy.

IV.5 Eudaimonic perspectives

Eudaimonic theories are rooted in Aristotle's philosophy, where true happiness *(eudaimonia)* is not about fleeting pleasure but living a life of virtue and purpose. Modern philosophers, such as Julia Annas and Martha Nussbaum, continue this tradition by emphasizing the importance of self-realization, personal growth, and fulfilling one's potential in accordance with ethical principles.

* *Virtue and moral excellence:* According to this view, happiness stems from practicing virtues like courage, wisdom, and justice. A flourishing life results from aligning actions with one's true nature and moral values.

* *Purpose and meaning:* Unlike hedonistic theories, which prioritize pleasure, eudaimonic theories argue that finding a purpose, cultivating relationships, and contributing to the greater good are central to a meaningful life.

* *Challenges and growth:* Personal development often requires embracing challenges and discomfort as part of the journey toward fulfillment and authenticity.

IV.6 Existential and postmodern views

These perspectives shift the focus from universal definitions of happiness to subjective and context-dependent constructions of well-being.

* *Existentialism and self-construction* (Jean-Paul Sartre): Sartre's existentialism posits that individuals are radically free to define their essence through choices and actions. Happiness, in this view, emerges from authentically embracing one's freedom and accepting re-

sponsibility for creating a meaningful life, rather than adhering to societal norms or external expectations.

* *Authenticity vs. bad faith:* Authenticity involves living truthfully according to one's chosen values, while bad faith refers to self-deception or conforming to imposed roles that limit freedom.

* *Postmodernism and questioning universals* (Michel Foucault): Post-modern thinkers challenge the idea of universal paths to happiness. Foucault, for example, critiques how power structures and social norms shape definitions of happiness and individual desires.

* *Cultural and individual diversity:* Postmodernism emphasizes that happiness cannot be reduced to a singular definition; it is fluid, subjective, and influenced by historical and cultural contexts.

These views highlight the importance of individual choice, the constructed nature of meaning, and the critical examination of societal influences on personal happiness.

IV.7 Political and social dimensions

Happiness is increasingly viewed as a political matter. Theories of justice (e.g., John Rawls) incorporate happiness as part of broader considerations of fairness, equality, and societal well-being. There is growing interest in the role governments play in promoting the happiness of citizens, inspired by Bhutan's *Gross National Happiness* (GNH) model.

IV.8 Critiques and challenges

Some contemporary philosophers question the pursuit of happiness as a primary life goal, suggesting it may lead to dissatisfaction or even alienation. Figures like Slavoj Žižek critique consumerist approaches to happiness, arguing that the commodification of joy undermines authentic fulfillment.

Chapter V
Happiness in religion

The concept of happiness in religion is deeply intertwined with notions of purpose, morality, and connection to the divine. Across different religious traditions, happiness is often seen not just as a fleeting emotion but as a state of being that reflects spiritual fulfillment, ethical living, and harmony with the cosmos or God.

In many religious frameworks, true happiness is linked to spiritual growth and alignment with divine will. This perspective suggests that material pleasures are temporary, while deeper, lasting happiness comes from cultivating virtues, seeking God, or achieving enlightenment.

Christianity emphasizes joy through faith in God, love, and the pursuit of righteousness. The Beatitudes from Jesus' Sermon on the Mount highlight how qualities like humility and mercy lead to spiritual blessedness.

Islam views happiness as tied to submission to Allah and following His guidance. Eternal happiness is a reward in the afterlife, while inner peace in this life comes from obedience and trust in God.

Buddhism teaches that happiness arises from letting go of desires and attachments. The Noble Eightfold Path guides practitioners toward inner peace and enlightenment *(nirvana),* which represents the ultimate form of happiness.

Most religions associate happiness with living a virtuous life. Good deeds, compassion, and selflessness are pathways to contentment. Happiness is not just personal but collective—promoting the well-being of others enhances one's own sense of joy.

Hinduism emphasizes *dharma* (duty) and *karma* (action) as pathways to happiness. Living in accordance with one's role and responsibilities, and cultivating inner detachment, leads to spiritual satisfaction.

Judaism connects happiness to communal and individual adherence to God's commandments. *Simcha* (joy) is often celebrated in community rituals and festivals, reinforcing the idea that happiness is both personal and shared.

Many religious traditions envision ultimate happiness in the afterlife. Earthly happiness is seen as incomplete or a reflection of divine grace, with the promise of eternal joy after death for those who live righteously.

Christianity and Islam both depict paradise as a place of eternal happiness and reward for the faithful. This perspective can provide hope and comfort in the face of suffering.

Hinduism and Buddhism focus on liberation from the cycle of rebirth *(moksha* or *nirvana)* as the highest form of happiness, transcending the limitations of worldly existence.

Religious practices, such as prayer, meditation, and communal worship, foster a sense of connection to the divine and to others. This collective aspect of religion brings joy through shared purpose and belonging.

Festivals, rituals, and sacred gatherings often serve as expressions of communal happiness, reinforcing bonds between individuals and their faith community.

Pilgrimages and spiritual journeys, found in many religions, offer profound experiences of happiness by reconnecting believers with sacred places and stories.

Religions also recognize the role of suffering in shaping happiness. Difficulties are seen as opportunities for growth, deeper faith, and eventual joy. The idea of redemptive suffering is present in Christianity (through Christ's sacrifice) and in Buddhism (suffering as a teacher leading to enlightenment).

V.1 Happiness in Judaism[10]

In Judaism, the concept of happiness (שמחה – *simcha)* is deeply rooted in spiritual, communal, and ethical dimensions. Jewish thought perceives happiness not just as fleeting joy, but as a state intertwined with purpose, gratitude, and connection to God *(Hashem),* community, and moral living.

V.1.1 Happiness as a *mitzvah* (commandment)

Judaism emphasizes the idea that joy is not merely an emotional state but a spiritual duty. The Torah instructs to *"serve the Lord with joy"* (Psalm 100:2). This reflects the belief that happiness is integral to religious practice and spiritual fulfillment.

[10] Judaism is one of the oldest monotheistic religions, originating in the ancient Near East (2000–1500 BCE). It traces its roots to Abraham, regarded as the first patriarch.

V.1.2 Gratitude and contentment

Jewish teachings encourage cultivating happiness through gratitude. Pirkei Avot *(Ethics of the Fathers)* 4:1 asks, *"Who is rich? He who rejoices in his portion."* This highlights that happiness stems from appreciating life's blessings rather than constant pursuit of material wealth.

V.1.3 Community and celebration

Judaism places great value on communal joy, especially during festivals. Weddings, *bat mitzvahs,* and holidays are marked by *simcha,* reinforcing the belief that happiness grows through shared experiences.

V.1.4 Moral and spiritual fulfillment

Happiness in Judaism often arises from fulfilling moral obligations and living a life aligned with divine values. Acts of kindness and charity are seen as pathways to true happiness, benefiting both the giver and receiver.

V.1.5 Balancing joy and suffering

Judaism acknowledges that life includes both joy and hardship. The Talmud teaches that even during moments of grief, one can maintain an undercurrent of hope and happiness. This balance is symbolized at weddings by breaking a glass, reminding of the destruction of the Temple even at the height of celebration.

V.1.6 Rabbinic perspectives

* *Maimonides (Rambam):* Described happiness as the result of intellectual and spiritual pursuit. He believed joy comes from engaging with Torah and aligning with divine wisdom.

* *Rabbi Nachman of Breslov:* Famously taught, "It is a great mitzvah to always be happy." Nachman emphasized that overcoming despair through joy is a crucial part of spiritual growth.

V.1.7 Joy in the face of challenges

The Jewish people's collective history of resilience reflects an ability to find joy even in adversity. This enduring sense of happiness and hope, often through humor and faith, underscores the Jewish approach to life's trials.

V.1.8 Practical applications

* Engaging in prayer, singing, and dancing during religious celebrations.
* Performing acts of kindness and fostering gratitude.
* Seeking joy in Torah study and spiritual practice.
* Embracing life's simple pleasures and fostering community bonds.

V.2 Happiness by Jewish theologians

Jewish theologians have explored the concept of happiness, or *simcha,* emphasizing its significance in spiritual life and its attainment through various practices.

Rabbi Schneur Zalman of Liadi (1745–1812), the founder of Chabad Hasidism, taught that joy arises from contemplating the unity of God. By deeply reflecting on this unity, individuals can elevate their spirits and achieve a state of happiness.

Rabbi Menachem Mendel Schneersohn (1789–1866), the third Chabad Rebbe, believed that adopting the demeanor of a joyful person, even when not genuinely feeling it, can lead to true happiness. He posited that actions influence emotions; thus, behaving joyfully can cultivate genuine joy.

Rabbi Nachman of Breslov (1772–1810) emphasized the importance of actively pursuing happiness. He taught that even feigned happiness has the power to transform one's personal situation, eventually leading to authentic joy.

In Hasidic thought, joy is considered essential. The Baal Shem Tov, founder of Hasidism, interpreted the verse "Serve God with happiness" to mean that the happiness itself is one's service to God. This perspective underscores the belief that joy is not merely a byproduct of religious observance but a fundamental component of divine service.

Additionally, the Hebrew Bible uses the term *Ashrei,* a plural form meaning "the happinesses of," suggesting that happiness is multifaceted, encompassing feelings, emotions, states of mind, and life judgments. This plurality indicates that happiness in Judaism is a composite of various positive experiences and states.

These teachings highlight that in Jewish thought, happiness is both a spiritual goal and a means to enhance one's connection with the divine.

V.3 Happiness in Christianity

Happiness in Christianity is deeply intertwined with spiritual fulfillment, divine relationship, and the pursuit of a virtuous life. Unlike secular definitions that often focus on personal pleasure or material success, Christian happiness is rooted in a relationship with God, the experience of grace, and the practice of love, humility, and service.

V.3.1 The source of happiness: God and Christ

In Christianity, true happiness is believed to come from God. The Psalms frequently reflect this:

"Happy are the people whose God is the Lord" (Psalm 144:15).

Jesus' teachings emphasize that happiness (often translated as "blessedness") is not about external circumstances but about inner peace and righteousness. The Beatitudes (Matthew 5:3-12) outline a countercultural vision of happiness—those who are poor in spirit, mourn, are meek, and hunger for righteousness are considered "blessed."

V.3.2 Happiness through relationship and grace

Christianity teaches that happiness flows from reconciliation with God through Christ. St. Augustine famously wrote: *"You have made us for yourself, O Lord, and our heart is restless until it rests in you."*

This suggests that happiness comes from aligning one's life with God's will, experiencing divine love, and trusting in His providence.

V.3.3 Joy vs. temporary happiness

Christianity often distinguishes between joy and fleeting happiness. Joy is seen as a deeper, more enduring state of well-being that persists even in suffering. The Apostle Paul, who faced significant hardships, wrote:

"Rejoice in the Lord always. I will say it again: Rejoice!" (Philippians 4:4).

This reflects the belief that joy arises from faith, hope, and love, even amid difficulties.

V.3.4 Moral and ethical happiness

Christian happiness is linked to living a moral and ethical life. Jesus' command to *"love your neighbor as yourself"* (Mark 12:31) implies that happiness is connected to compassion, forgiveness, and community. Acts of kindness and selflessness are seen as pathways to deeper contentment.

V.3.5 Eternal perspective: The kingdom of heaven

For Christians, ultimate happiness is tied to the hope of eternal life. Earthly happiness is considered temporary, while true fulfillment awaits believers in the presence of God. This eschatological hope influences how Christians view suffering and hardship, reinforcing the belief that earthly trials are temporary steps toward eternal joy.

V.3.6 Practical expressions of happiness in Christian life

* *Worship and prayer* – Communion with God brings spiritual joy.

* *Community and fellowship* – Shared faith fosters collective happiness and support.

* *Service and charity* – Serving others leads to a sense of purpose and fulfillment.

**Forgiveness and healing* – Letting go of bitterness and embracing grace promotes inner peace.

V.4 Happiness by different Christian theologians

Different Christian theologians have approached the idea of happiness from diverse angles, blending scriptural insights with philosophical traditions, particularly those of ancient Greek thinkers like Aristotle and Plato. Below is a development of this idea through key theological figures and concepts.

V.4.1 Biblical foundations

In the Bible, happiness (often translated as "blessedness") is linked to living in accordance with God's will.

* *Old Testament:* Happiness is often associated with obedience to God's law (Psalm 1:1-3), trust in God (Proverbs 16:20), and the fear of the Lord (Proverbs 28:14).

* *New Testament:* Jesus' Beatitudes (Matthew 5:3-12) redefine happiness as spiritual flourishing rooted in humility, mercy, and peacemaking. This happiness transcends worldly circumstances and points to the Kingdom of Heaven.

V.4.2 St. Augustine (354–430) – Happiness in God alone

Augustine argued that true happiness cannot be found in material goods or earthly pleasures but only in God. In his works, such as *Confessions* and *The City of God,* he develops the idea that humanity's restless heart finds peace only in God.

Key concept: "Our hearts are restless until they rest in You" (Confessions, I.1).

Happiness is ultimately the enjoyment of God, and the highest form of happiness is the beatific vision—seeing God face to face in eternity.

V.4.3 Thomas Aquinas (1225–1274) – Beatitudo and perfect Happiness

Aquinas, heavily influenced by Aristotle, distinguished between two types of happiness:

* *Imperfect happiness (felicitas)* – attainable on earth through virtuous living and the natural pursuit of wisdom.

* *Perfect happiness* (beatitudo) – achievable only in the afterlife, in the direct knowledge and love of God.

Aquinas argued that while virtuous living brings a measure of happiness, ultimate happiness is union with God, which surpasses natural human capacity and requires divine grace.

V.4.4 Medieval mystics – Experiencing happiness through union with God

Figures like St. Teresa of Ávila and St. John of the Cross emphasized mystical experiences of happiness through direct, intimate union with God.

This form of happiness often involves suffering and purification, but results in a deep spiritual joy that anticipates heavenly bliss.

V.4.5 Reformation thinkers – Happiness and grace

Reformers like Martin Luther and John Calvin placed happiness in the context of divine grace and justification by faith.

For Luther, happiness comes from trusting in God's promises and experiencing the freedom of salvation.

Calvin linked happiness to the sovereignty of God and the believer's sense of assurance in God's providential care.

V.4.6 Contemporary theological approaches

Modern Christian theologians often focus on happiness in the context of social justice, community, and holistic well-being. Figures like N.T. Wright explore happiness as part of the Kingdom of God, realized partially now and fully in the age to come.

Happiness is seen as a byproduct of living in alignment with the values of love, justice, and reconciliation.

V.4.7 Summary of key themes in Christian theology of happiness

* *God as the source of true happiness:* According to Christian theology, earthly pleasures and material gains, while temporarily satisfying, are fleeting and insufficient for ultimate fulfillment. True and lasting happiness is found only in God, who is the supreme good and the origin of all joy and contentment.

* *Virtue and grace:* Genuine happiness involves living a life of virtue — cultivating moral character, righteousness, and love. However, human effort alone is inadequate for attaining the fullness of happiness. Divine grace, freely given by God, is essential for elevating human nature and perfecting the pursuit of moral goodness.

* *Eternal perspective:* The complete and perfect state of happiness is not achievable in this earthly life. It lies beyond death, in the beatific vision — the direct encounter and eternal enjoyment of God in heaven. This eternal perspective shapes Christian understanding of hope and perseverance.

* *Communal and personal dimensions:* While happiness is deeply personal, it is also communal. Flourishing as a Christian involves loving others, participating in the life of the Church, and contributing to the well-being of the larger body of Christ. Authentic happiness reflects the interconnectedness of human relationships rooted in divine love.

V.5 Happiness in Islam

Happiness in Islam is a profound and multi-dimensional concept that extends beyond fleeting pleasures and material satisfaction. It intertwines the physical, spiritual, emotional, and social aspects of life, grounded in the belief that true contentment arises from a harmonious relationship with God (Allah), oneself, and others.

V.5.1 Spiritual Fulfillment

In Islam, the heart is central to happiness. A "sound heart" is one free from spiritual diseases like envy, arrogance, and hatred. Inner peace is achieved through remembrance of God, prayer, and sincere devotion. The Qur'an highlights:

"Verily, in the remembrance of Allah do hearts find rest." (Qur'an 13:28).

V.5.2 Key practices for spiritual happiness

* *Daily prayers* – Direct communication with God.
* *Fasting* – Purification of the soul and increased empathy.
* *Charity* – Fulfilling social responsibilities and finding joy in giving.

V.5.3 Purpose and meaning

Islam teaches that happiness is rooted in living a purposeful life aligned with divine guidance. This involves striving for excellence in worship and conduct, and cultivating God-consciousness. When individuals align their actions with higher moral and spiritual goals, they experience fulfillment and clarity.

"And I did not create the jinn and mankind except to worship Me." (Qur'an 51:56)

Happiness in this sense is tied to knowing one's role in the world and pursuing the pleasure of God. The joy of serving a higher cause transcends worldly distractions.

V.5.4 Balance and moderation

Islam emphasizes balance in all aspects of life – between worship and worldly affairs, work and family, body and soul. The Qur'an describes the Muslim community as a *"justly balanced nation"*.

Excessive indulgence or asceticism can disrupt happiness, but moderation fosters holistic well-being.

"And seek, by means of what Allah has given you, the Hereafter, but do not forget your share in the world." (Qur'an 28:77)

V.5.5 Social bonds and community

Islam views happiness as interconnected with the well-being of others. Acts of kindness, compassion, and maintaining family ties enhance collective joy. The Prophet Muhammad (PBUH) said:

"None of you truly believes until he loves for his brother what he loves for himself." (Bukhari, *Muslim)*

Building strong communities, fostering forgiveness, and resolving conflicts contribute to societal happiness and unity.

V.5.6 Contentment

Islamic teachings encourage gratitude *(shukr)* and patience *(ṣabr)* as keys to contentment. True happiness is found not in accumulating wealth but in appreciating blessings and trusting in God's plan *(tawakkul)*.

"Richness is not having many possessions, but true richness is the richness of the soul." (Bukhari, *Muslim)*

V.5.7 Eternal perspective

Islamic happiness is deeply tied to the afterlife *(ākhirah).* Believers find solace in the hope of eternal bliss in Paradise *(Jannah).* This long-term view helps individuals endure hardships with optimism and resilience.

"Whoever does righteousness, whether male or female, while believing – We will surely grant them a good life." (Qur'an 16:97)

The ultimate joy lies in the vision of God *(ru'yat Allah)* in the Hereafter, representing the pinnacle of happiness for the believer.

V.6 Happiness by Muslim theologians

Muslim theologians have historically approached the concept of happiness in a manner that integrates spiritual, ethical, and worldly dimensions. Their perspectives are deeply rooted in Islamic teachings from the Qur'an, *Hadith* (sayings of Prophet Muhammad, peace be upon him), and the works of classical scholars.

V.6.1 Definitions and types of happiness

Muslim thinkers often distinguish between different types of happiness:

* *Worldly happiness:* Linked to material well-being, family life, health, and success. It is recognized but not seen as the ultimate goal.

* *Spiritual or eternal happiness*: The true and ultimate form of happiness, associated with proximity to Allah and eternal bliss in the Hereafter.

The balance between these two types of happiness is emphasized throughout Islamic teachings.

V.6.1.1 Al-Ghazali

Al-Ghazali discusses happiness in depth in *Iḥyāʾ ʿulūm al-dīn (The revival of the religious sciences):*

He defines true happiness as the result of knowledge of God and moral refinement.

Happiness is linked to purifying the soul from worldly desires and cultivating virtues like patience, gratitude, and sincerity.

The ultimate form of happiness comes from direct knowledge and love of Allah, leading to inner peace and spiritual contentment.

V.6.1.2 Ibn Sina

As a philosopher and theologian, Ibn Sina approached happiness from a metaphysical and rational standpoint:

He argued that happiness is linked to the soul's perfection through intellectual and spiritual development.

True happiness comes from aligning human will with divine will and pursuing knowledge of higher truths.

V.6.1.3 Ibn al-Qayyim (1292–1350 CE)

In his works, such as *Madārij al-sālikīn (The stations of the seekers),* Ibn al-Qayyim emphasizes:

Happiness is the outcome of a close relationship with Allah, achieved through worship, repentance, and *dhikr* (remembrance of God).

He stresses that worldly pleasures are temporary, while the joy of obedience to Allah leads to lasting satisfaction.

V.6.2 Qur'anic and prophetic foundations

Many Qur'anic verses and sayings of the Prophet (PBUH) provide guidance on achieving happiness:

Qur'an 13:28: *"Verily, in the remembrance of Allah do hearts find rest."*

Hadith: *"True enrichment does not come through possessing a lot of wealth, but true enrichment is the enrichment of the soul."*

V.6.3 Practical approaches to happiness

Muslim theologians propose several practical means to attain happiness:

* *Developing a strong relationship with Allah through prayer, reflection, and worship.*

* *Cultivating virtue:* Patience, humility, gratitude, and kindness are seen as keys to contentment.

* *Focusing on the Hereafter:* Viewing this life as temporary encourages a focus on actions that lead to eternal bliss.

* *Moderation and balance*: Pursuing permissible worldly pleasures without excess and maintaining spiritual obligations.

V.6.4 Happiness as a communal concept

Islamic teachings extend happiness to include communal welfare:

Zakāt (charity) and *ṣadāqah* (voluntary giving) bring happiness by reducing societal inequality.

Acts of kindness and compassion are central to creating a happy, harmonious society.

Chapter VI
Happiness in literature

The concept of happiness has been a central theme in literature across cultures and time periods, serving as a lens through which authors explore human existence, societal norms, and individual aspirations.

VI.1 Classical and philosophical perspectives

Ancient texts: In classical literature, happiness is often tied to virtues, morality, and alignment with cosmic or divine order. Aristotle's concept of *eudaimonia* (flourishing or living well) as the ultimate human goal finds echoes in literature of the time.

Example: In Homer's *Odyssey,* Odysseus's happiness is linked to his return home, where personal fulfillment and the restoration of social order intertwine.

Religious texts: Many religious works, like the Bible, Quran, or Hindu scriptures, depict happiness as spiritual fulfillment, often achievable through devotion, selflessness, or alignment with divine will.

VI.2 Enlightenment and rational pursuits

During the Age of Enlightenment[11] happiness began to be associated with reason, individual freedom, and societal progress. Literature from this era reflects these shifts, advocating for human agency in crafting personal joy.

Example: In Voltaire's *Candide,* the pursuit of happiness is satirized, ultimately suggesting that cultivating one's own garden (metaphorically living simply and productively) is key to contentment.

VI.3 Romanticism and emotional fulfillment

The Romantic period (c. 1780 – 1850) emphasized emotional depth, individuality, and the connection between happiness and nature. Romantic writers often framed happiness as a fleeting, elusive state tied to passion and imagination.

Example: In Wordsworth's poetry, happiness is found in the sublime beauty of nature and introspection, as seen in *"Lines Composed a Few Miles Above Tintern Abbey."*

VI.4 Victorian and realist perspectives

In Victorian[12] literature, happiness often intersects with societal expectations, morality, and class structures. Realist writers, on the other hand, explore happiness in the face of life's complexities and imperfections.

---

[11] The Age of Enlightenment or the Age of Reason was an intellectual and cultural movement that began in the late 17th century and peaked in the 18th century, primarily in Europe.

[12] The Victorian era, coinciding with the reign of Queen Victoria (1837–1901).

Example: In Jane Austen's *Pride and Prejudice,* happiness is achieved through self-awareness and overcoming social constraints, particularly in relationships.

VI.5 Modernism and existential reflections

Modernist literature frequently questions the traditional constructs of happiness, reflecting disillusionment and the fragmented nature of modern life. Existentialism delves into the search for meaning in a seemingly indifferent universe.

Philosophers like Friedrich Nietzsche and Albert Camus present unique perspectives on happiness that diverge from traditional notions of pleasure or comfort. Instead of viewing happiness as the absence of suffering, they explore how confronting life's difficulties and embracing existential struggles can lead to deeper fulfillment and meaning.

Nietzsche's concept of happiness is intertwined with his idea of the will to power – the drive to grow, assert oneself, and overcome obstacles. For Nietzsche happiness comes through self-overcoming. By challenging one's limitations and striving for greatness, individuals cultivate a sense of vitality and fulfillment. He believed that enduring hardship and embracing discomfort fuels personal development, much like how fire tempers steel. He advocates for affirming life in its entirety, including suffering and tragedy. Accepting and loving all aspects of life, even the painful ones, fosters a profound and enduring form of happiness.

Albert Camus, a key figure in existentialist thought, approached happiness through the lens of absurdism – the recognition of life's inherent lack of meaning. Rather than succumbing to despair, Camus suggests embracing the absurd with defiance and joy.

In Camus' famous essay, *The Myth of Sisyphus,* he depicts Sisyphus endlessly pushing a boulder uphill. Camus argues that Sisyphus, by embracing his fate and finding contentment in the act itself, achieves a form of happiness.

Camus posits that happiness arises when individuals confront the absurdity of life and choose to live fully and passionately, despite the lack of inherent meaning.

By acknowledging life's uncertainties and choosing to engage deeply with experiences, individuals create their own sense of purpose and joy.

In Virginia Woolf's *Mrs. Dalloway,* fleeting moments of happiness are juxtaposed with existential crises, illustrating the transient and subjective nature of joy.

VI.6 Postmodernism and contemporary views

In the contemporary literary landscape, the conception of happiness has evolved into a multifaceted and nuanced theme. Moving beyond traditional, often universalized portrayals, modern writers engage with happiness as a complex, fluid, and deeply personal experience, shaped by cultural, social, and individual factors.

Postmodernist literature challenges the grand narratives and universal truths that once defined happiness in classical and modern literature. Writers in this tradition question whether happiness is achievable, stable, or even desirable within a fragmented and relativistic world. For instance, Don DeLillo's *White Noise* interrogates consumer culture's promise of happiness, exposing the emptiness underlying materialistic pursuits. Similarly, David Foster Wallace's *Infinite Jest* explores addiction and entertainment as false proxies for fulfillment, suggesting that the search for happiness is riddled with contradiction and self-deception. Postmodernist texts often emphasize the interplay between external societal pressures and internal struggles, leaving readers with an ambiguous, open-ended perspective on what happiness means in a fragmented era.

VI.7 Intersectionality: Happiness in the context of race, gender, and identity

Contemporary authors foreground intersectionality to explore how happiness is experienced differently depending on race, gender, and other aspects of identity. Toni Morrison's works, such as *Sula* and *Beloved,* delve into the ways systemic racism, historical trauma, and the resilience of Black communities shape their pursuit of joy and meaning. Morrison portrays happiness as an act of resistance and survival, often intertwined with memory and collective identity.

Similarly, Zadie Smith's *White Teeth* and *On Beauty* examine the intersections of race, immigration, and family dynamics, portraying happiness as a process negotiated through cultural hybridity and generational conflicts. In these works, happiness is rarely linear or simplistic; instead, it emerges as a negotiation between self-acceptance and societal expectations.

VI.8 Popular fiction: Self-discovery and happiness in contemporary novels

In popular fiction, the pursuit of happiness is frequently depicted as a journey of self-discovery. Bestselling novels like Elizabeth Gilbert's *Eat, Pray, Love* and Gail Honeyman's *Eleanor Oliphant Is Completely Fine* explore the quest for personal fulfillment in the wake of life's challenges. These narratives often emphasize the transformative power of self-reflection, connection, and resilience in achieving a sense of happiness.

In the young adult genre, works like John Green's *The Fault in Our Stars* and Angie Thomas's *The Hate U Give* balance the harsh realities of life with moments of joy and connection, portraying happiness as both fleeting and deeply meaningful. These stories resonate with readers by capturing the complexity of emotional growth and the universal desire for love, belonging, and purpose.

VI.9 Themes and patterns across eras

VI.9.1 The elusiveness of happiness

In literature, happiness is frequently depicted as fleeting, elusive, and often just out of reach. Many narratives suggest that happiness, rather than being a constant state, manifests in brief moments, shaped by circumstance and perspective. This impermanence mirrors real human experiences, where joy is punctuated by periods of hardship, growth, or reflection. Writers like F. Scott Fitzgerald in *The Great Gatsby* portray characters who chase after an idealized happiness, only to find it evanescent or illusory. Gatsby's relentless pursuit of Daisy, driven by his belief that she represents his ultimate happiness, underscores the fragility of such aspirations. Similarly, in *Of Mice and Men,* John Steinbeck illustrates how dreams of a better future provide fleeting glimpses of happiness, but these dreams are vulnerable to the harsh realities of life. Through these works, literature emphasizes that happiness is not a fixed destination but rather a series of transient experiences that shape and define the human condition.

VI.9.2 Interplay of individual and society

Happiness in literature is often examined through the lens of societal norms and constraints, reflecting the tension between personal desires and communal expectations. This theme highlights the complexities individuals face when their pursuit of happiness conflicts with societal roles or traditions. In *Pride and Prejudice* by Jane Austen, Elizabeth Bennet's happiness hinges on her ability to navigate the rigid social structures governing marriage and class. Her ultimate fulfillment comes from reconciling personal integrity with societal expectations. Similarly, George Orwell's *1984* explores how oppressive societies suppress individual joy, illustrating that personal happiness can be stifled or even manipulated by external forces. Literature suggests that while society can provide frameworks for joy and fulfillment, it can also impose barriers, making the pursuit of happiness a nuanced interplay between self and society.

VI.9.3 The role of nature, love, and art

Recurring motifs in literature highlight nature, love, and art as essential sources of happiness, often portrayed as intrinsic to the human experience. Love, as depicted in works such as *Romeo and*

Juliet by Shakespeare, offers both ecstatic happiness and devastating sorrow, demonstrating love's dual capacity to uplift and wound. Art, too, becomes a conduit for happiness, as seen in *The Picture of Dorian Gray* by Oscar Wilde, where beauty and artistic creation provide fleeting yet intense pleasures. These elements signify that while external achievements or material gains may offer temporary satisfaction, deeper and more enduring forms of happiness often stem from intimate connections with nature, love, and artistic expression.

Chapter VII
Happiness in American literature

The concept of happiness in American literature reflects the evolving cultural, social, and philosophical underpinnings of the nation throughout its history. From the pursuit of individual fulfillment in early colonial texts to the exploration of existential questions in contemporary works, American writers have consistently grappled with the meaning and attainability of happiness.

In early American literature, happiness was often linked to religious and communal ideals. Puritan writers like Jonathan Edwards expressed happiness as a spiritual condition, achievable through piety and alignment with divine will. Similarly, early settlers and colonial writers portrayed happiness as a collective goal, rooted in the success and survival of the community. This communal notion of happiness gradually evolved with the rise of individualism during the Enlightenment and Revolutionary periods. *The Declaration of Independence*, penned by Thomas Jefferson, famously enshrined "the pursuit of happiness" as an inalienable right, reflecting the growing emphasis on personal liberty and self-determination.

The 19th century saw American literature broaden its depiction of happiness, reflecting the complexities of personal ambition and societal constraints. Writers such as Ralph Waldo Emerson and Henry David Thoreau explored happiness through the lens of transcendentalism, advocating for a return to nature, self-reliance, and the inner journey toward fulfillment. In contrast, Nathaniel Hawthorne and Herman Melville depicted happiness as elusive, often obstructed by human flaws, societal norms, and moral dilemmas.

During the late 19th and early 20th centuries, the rise of industrialization and urbanization brought new dimensions to the literary exploration of happiness. Realist and naturalist writers like Mark Twain, Edith Wharton, and Theodore Dreiser questioned the attainability of happiness in a rapidly changing society marked by economic disparity and social upheaval. Twain's satire often highlighted the false promises of material wealth, while Wharton exposed the limitations imposed by rigid social hierarchies.

The Modernist period further complicated the literary pursuit of happiness, as writers like F. Scott Fitzgerald and Ernest Hemingway depicted characters disillusioned by the emptiness of the American Dream. Hemingway's sparse prose often reflects a stoic resignation to life's inherent struggles, suggesting that happiness lies in fleeting moments of connection and personal integrity.

In contemporary American literature, the concept of happiness continues to be multifaceted, shaped by issues of identity, race, gender, and mental health. Authors such as Toni Morrison, Jhumpa Lahiri, and Chimamanda Ngozi Adichie explore the intersections of happiness with cultural heritage, displacement, and the search for belonging. Morrison's works, for example, highlight the resilience and joy found within marginalized communities despite historical trauma.

Overall, happiness in American literature serves as a mirror to the nation's evolving ethos, reflecting both its aspirations and its disillusionments. From the collective hopes of early settlers to the personal quests of modern individuals, the pursuit of happiness remains a central, enduring theme that continues to inspire and challenge American writers and readers alike.

Chapter VIII
Happiness in English literature

VIII.1 Happiness in classical and medieval literature

VIII.1.1 Beowulf and the heroic ideal: Happiness through honor and legacy

In the epic poem *Beowulf,* happiness is inextricably linked to the pursuit of honor, valor, and the establishment of a lasting legacy. For the Anglo-Saxon warrior culture depicted in the text, personal fulfillment and societal respect are achieved through acts of bravery, loyalty, and service to one's people. Beowulf's battles against Grendel, Grendel's mother, and the dragon serve not only to protect his kingdom but also to cement his reputation as a noble and courageous leader. The concept of happiness in Beowulf aligns with the idea of achieving glory in life and securing remembrance in death. The poem suggests that true happiness is found in the pursuit of deeds that benefit the greater community and ensure the continuation of one's name long after physical demise. This notion of happiness is communal and deeply tied to the warrior code of honor.

VIII.1.2 Chaucer's The Canterbury Tales: Pursuit of happiness through morality and pilgrimage

Geoffrey Chaucer's *The Canterbury Tales* presents a diverse exploration of happiness, reflecting the varied social strata and personal values of medieval society. The characters' pilgrimage to Canterbury symbolizes a collective yet individual pursuit of spiritual and earthly fulfillment. For some, happiness is rooted in moral integrity and religious devotion, while others seek pleasure through storytelling, wealth, or romantic conquests. The Knight, for example, represents the chivalric ideal, finding joy in his adherence to the principles of honor and justice. Conversely, the Wife of Bath finds happiness in personal autonomy and marital experience. Chaucer's work highlights the multiplicity of paths to happiness, suggesting that morality, social engagement, and the pursuit of personal desires all contribute to the complex tapestry of medieval life. The pilgrimage itself becomes a metaphor for the journey towards happiness, underscoring the importance of introspection and community in achieving personal contentment.

VIII.1.3 Medieval literature's focus on divine happiness and spiritual fulfillment

A significant theme in medieval literature is the belief that ultimate happiness resides in divine grace and spiritual fulfillment. Texts such as *The Divine Comedy* by Dante Alighieri emphasize the soul's journey towards eternal bliss in the presence of God. In this context, earthly joys are seen as fleeting, while true happiness is eternal and derived from alignment with divine will. Religious allegories, hagiographies, and mystical writings of the period reinforce the idea that human life is a pilgrimage towards salvation. Figures such as St. Augustine, in his *Confessions,* reflect on the transient nature of worldly pleasures and the enduring peace found in spiritual enlightenment. This perspective posits that happiness is not merely a personal or social pursuit but a sacred endeavor that transcends temporal existence and leads to unity with the divine.

Together, these works reveal that classical and medieval literature view happiness as a multifaceted concept shaped by cultural, social, and religious ideals. Whether through the heroism of *Beowulf,* the moral and social narratives of *The Canterbury Tales,* or the divine aspirations of spiritual texts, the pursuit of happiness in these eras reflects a profound engagement with questions of purpose, legacy, and the nature of fulfillment.

VIII.1.4 Renaissance and enlightenment perspectives

VIII.1.4.1 Shakespeare's exploration of personal joy and tragedy

William Shakespeare's works frequently navigate the interplay between joy and tragedy, illustrating the fluidity of human emotion and the fragility of happiness. In comedies like *As You Like It* and *Much Ado About Nothing,* Shakespeare presents joy as a dynamic and often fleeting experience, shaped by misunderstanding, disguise, and ultimately reconciliation.

In *As You Like It,* characters find joy through escape and transformation in the Forest of Arden. Rosalind, disguised as Ganymede, orchestrates romantic unions, fostering an environment where personal growth and love flourish. This pastoral setting symbolizes the potential for renewal and joy, contrasting with the constraints of court life. However, the presence of melancholic characters such as Jaques underscores the precariousness of happiness, highlighting Shakespeare's nuanced perspective that joy is not absolute but rather a state balanced with underlying sorrow.

Similarly, *Much Ado About Nothing* explores the tension between joy and personal tragedy. Benedick and Beatrice's witty exchanges exemplify the delight found in verbal sparring and romantic pursuit, yet their path to happiness is obstructed by deception and the near-tragic downfall of Hero. Ultimately, Shakespeare's resolution of these conflicts affirms the redemptive power of love and community, suggesting that joy, while vulnerable to disruption, can prevail through resilience and understanding.

VIII.1.4.2 Milton's Paradise Lost – happiness and the fall from grace

John Milton's *Paradise Lost* offers a profound meditation on the nature of happiness and the consequences of its loss. The epic poem recounts the fall of Adam and Eve, illustrating how disobedience and pride lead to the forfeiture of paradise and the introduction of suffering into the human condition.

Milton presents happiness in *Paradise Lost* as synonymous with divine obedience and unity with God. Adam and Eve's existence in Eden reflects an idyllic joy rooted in innocence and mutual love. However, the serpent's temptation and their subsequent transgression result in exile, underscoring the fragility of this bliss. Through the fall, Milton conveys that happiness is inextricably linked to virtue and that its loss serves as a poignant reminder of humanity's inherent imperfection.

Despite the tragic narrative, *Paradise Lost* concludes with a message of hope and redemption. Adam and Eve's acceptance of their mortality and commitment to perseverance reflect Milton's belief in the possibility of finding contentment and grace through repentance and faith, even in a fallen world.

VIII.1.4.3 Enlightenment writers – Rationality, contentment, and the pursuit of virtue

Enlightenment thinkers, including Alexander Pope, emphasized the role of reason, virtue, and the pursuit of moral clarity in achieving happiness. Pope's *An Essay on Man* articulates the idea that contentment arises from accepting one's place in the "Great Chain of Being" and recognizing the inherent order and purpose within the universe.

Pope advocates for humility and self-awareness, urging readers to align their desires with rational thought and divine providence. The Enlightenment perspective posits that happiness stems not from the pursuit of pleasure but from the cultivation of virtue and the acceptance of life's limitations. This rational approach contrasts with the emotional intensity of Renaissance literature, reflecting a shift toward intellectual and ethical frameworks for understanding joy and fulfillment.

VIII.1.4.4 Romanticism and the search for emotional fulfillment

The Romantic period marked a shift towards an emphasis on individual emotion, nature, and the sublime as central elements of happiness and personal fulfillment. Key figures such as William Wordsworth, John Keats, and Percy Bysshe Shelley explored the profound connection between the natural world and the inner life, presenting nature as a restorative and inspirational force. For Wordsworth, nature was a teacher and a source of spiritual renewal, as seen in works like *Lines Composed a Few Miles above Tintern Abbey,* where he reflects on the calming and uplifting influence of the landscape. Similarly, Keats's *Ode to a Nightingale* reveals a yearning for transcendence through nature's beauty, while Shelley's *Ode to the West Wind* celebrates the transformative power of the natural world.

Romanticism also emphasized the sublime—a concept that merges awe, beauty, and a sense of the infinite. The sublime allowed individuals to experience profound emotional responses that could lead to personal growth and happiness. The pursuit of happiness in Romantic literature was not limited to external conditions but deeply tied to one's internal capacity to engage with and interpret experiences. This belief elevated imagination as a key faculty in constructing happiness. Through imaginative engagement, Romantic poets believed one could transcend the limitations of ordinary life, experiencing moments of intense joy and insight.

VIII.1.4.5 Victorian literature: The social and moral dimensions of happiness

Victorian literature reflects a more complex and often somber exploration of happiness, shaped by rapid industrialization, social inequality, and evolving moral frameworks. Writers like Charles Dickens used their works to highlight the importance of empathy, social responsibility, and the moral imperative to foster happiness in others. In *A Christmas Carol,* Dickens illustrates how personal transformation and generosity lead to a more fulfilling and joyful life, reinforcing the idea that happiness is intertwined with social justice and compassion.

The Brontë sisters, particularly Charlotte and Emily, examined the tension between personal desires and societal constraints. In *Jane Eyre,* Charlotte Brontë's protagonist struggles to balance her quest for personal happiness with the rigid social norms of the time. Similarly, Emily Brontë's *Wuthering Heights* portrays a passionate but destructive pursuit of happiness, reflecting the challenges of reconciling individual longing with external limitations.

Thomas Hardy, on the other hand, presented a more pessimistic view of happiness, often depicting it as fragile and fleeting. In novels like *Tess of the d'Urbervilles* and *Jude the Obscure,* Hardy explores the harsh realities of fate, societal pressures, and personal misfortune, suggesting that happiness is frequently undermined by forces beyond human control.

Together, Romantic and Victorian literature offer a rich and varied exploration of happiness, revealing how its pursuit is shaped by personal, societal, and existential factors across different literary periods.

VIII.1.4.6 Modernism and the fragmentation of happiness

Modernism, as a literary and cultural movement of the late 19th and early 20th centuries, was deeply marked by the upheavals of war, industrialization, and rapid social change. The concept of happiness, once a clear and attainable goal, became increasingly elusive, fragmented, and subjective. Modernist writers often explored happiness not as a universal state but as a deeply personal, often fleeting experience, fractured by the alienation and disillusionment of the modern world.

VIII.1.4.6.1 Virginia Woolf and James Joyce – Internal, subjective happiness

Virginia Woolf and James Joyce, two of the most celebrated modernist novelists, delved into the inner workings of the human mind to depict happiness as a subjective and transient experience.

Virginia Woolf: In works like *Mrs. Dalloway* and *To the Lighthouse,* Woolf used stream-of-consciousness narrative techniques to explore her characters' internal worlds. Happiness, in Woolf's vision, is often ephemeral and tied to moments of perception or connection, such as Clarissa Dalloway's joy in the ordinary act of buying flowers or Lily Briscoe's satisfaction in completing her painting. These moments are imbued with a sense of fragility, as they exist alongside the persistent undercurrents of loss and uncertainty.

James Joyce: Similarly, Joyce's *Ulysses* portrays happiness as fragmented and interwoven with the mundane. Through the detailed interior monologues of characters like Leopold Bloom, Joyce highlights the small, private pleasures—eating a meal, reminiscing about a loved one, or enjoying a moment of solitude. Yet, these moments of joy are juxtaposed against the broader chaos and isolation of urban life in early 20th-century Dublin.

VIII.1.4.6.2 T.S. Eliot's The Waste Land – The difficulty of finding happiness in a fractured world

T.S. Eliot's seminal poem *The Waste Land* encapsulates the modernist skepticism about happiness in an era of cultural and spiritual disintegration. The poem's fragmented structure, shifting voices, and allusions to myth and history reflect a world in pieces. Happiness in *The Waste Land* is almost entirely absent, overshadowed by themes of despair, disconnection, and existential dread. Any hope for joy is fleeting, as seen in the desperate yearning for renewal in lines like "Shantih shantih shantih," a Sanskrit invocation for peace. Eliot's vision underscores the profound challenges of finding contentment in a world ravaged by war and bereft of shared meaning.

VIII.1.4.7 Modernist skepticism about happiness in the face of war and industrialization

The horrors of World War I, the alienation wrought by industrialization, and the erosion of traditional values shaped a modernist worldview that questioned the very possibility of enduring happiness. The rapid pace of technological and societal change created a sense of instability, leaving individuals to grapple with feelings of isolation and loss. Modernist literature often portrays happiness as fractured—something to be pursued within the confines of individual experience rather than through collective or external means.

Chapter IX
Happiness in French literature

The concept of happiness in French literature is a multifaceted theme that has evolved over centuries, reflecting shifts in philosophical, social, and personal perspectives. From classical to contemporary works, happiness has been portrayed as a complex and often elusive ideal. Below is an exploration of how French literature has developed this theme through different periods:

IX.1 Classical and enlightenment era

* *Renaissance and humanism:* During the Renaissance, authors like Michel de Montaigne explored happiness as a personal and philosophical pursuit. In his Essais, Montaigne advocates for a life rooted in balance, self-reflection, and the enjoyment of simple pleasures.

* E*nlightenment philosophy:* The Enlightenment emphasized reason, progress, and the pursuit of happiness as a societal and individual goal. Voltaire's *Candide* critiques naive optimism, epitomized by Pangloss's belief that "all is for the best in the best of all possible worlds." Ultimately, the novel suggests that cultivating one's garden—finding contentment in practical work and modest living—leads to true happiness.

IX.2 Romanticism and the pursuit of emotional fulfillment

Romanticism marked a shift toward the inner life and emotional intensity. Authors like Victor Hugo and Alphonse de Lamartine delved into the joy and suffering of the human heart. Hugo's *Les Misérables* presents happiness as an aspiration intertwined with justice, love, and redemption.

Lamartine's poetry, particularly in *Méditations poétiques,* often portrays happiness as fleeting and tied to nature's beauty and personal reflection, though shadowed by melancholy.

IX.3 Realism and naturalism

In the 19th century, Realist authors like Gustave Flaubert explored happiness in the context of societal constraints. *Madame Bovary* is a poignant example of the disillusionment that can follow unrealistic expectations of happiness.

Naturalist writers like Émile Zola analyzed happiness within the deterministic framework of heredity and environment. In works like *L'Assommoir,* happiness is portrayed as a fragile state, often crushed by societal forces.

IX.4 Existentialism and modern perspectives

Existentialist literature of the 20th century, led by figures like Jean-Paul Sartre and Albert Camus, redefined happiness in a world perceived as absurd. In Camus's *L'Étranger* and *Le Mythe de Sisyphe,* happiness emerges as an act of defiance, a conscious embrace of life's struggles.

Simone de Beauvoir's writings, such as *The Second Sex,* explore the intersection of freedom, identity, and happiness, particularly in the context of gender roles and existential authenticity.

IX.5 Postmodern and contemporary views

Contemporary French literature often examines happiness in a fragmented, globalized world. Authors like Michel Houellebecq critique modernity's promises of happiness, highlighting themes of alienation and the commodification of pleasure.

Conversely, writers such as Philippe Delerm *(La première gorgée de bière)* celebrate small, everyday joys, presenting happiness as accessible through mindfulness and appreciation of the mundane.

Chapter X
Happiness in German literature

In German literature, the exploration of happiness often reflects the broader philosophical, social, and historical currents of the time. From Enlightenment optimism to Romantic longing and existential questioning, the portrayal of happiness evolves, offering readers insight into the German intellectual landscape.

X.1 Enlightenment and rational happiness

During the German Enlightenment of the 18th century, happiness was closely tied to reason, progress, and self-improvement. Thinkers like Immanuel Kant and Gotthold Ephraim Lessing believed that the pursuit of knowledge and moral virtue led to individual and collective happiness. Lessing's play *Nathan der Weise (Nathan the Wise)* exemplifies this belief, advocating for religious tolerance and rational discourse as pathways to harmony and fulfillment.

Johann Wolfgang von Goethe's *Wilhelm Meister's Apprenticeship (Wilhelm Meisters Lehrjahre)* reflects this Enlightenment ideal through the protagonist's journey of self-discovery and personal development. Wilhelm seeks happiness through artistic ambition and practical engagement with the world, mirroring Goethe's belief in self-cultivation as essential to a fulfilled life.

X.2 Romanticism and the longing for happiness

The Romantic period, spanning the late 18th and early 19th centuries, introduced a more emotional and subjective approach to happiness. German Romantics like Novalis, Friedrich Hölderlin, and E.T.A. Hoffmann emphasized the transcendental and often unattainable nature of true happiness. In Novalis' *Hymns to the Night (Hymnen an die Nacht),* happiness appears intertwined with mysticism and a longing for unity with the infinite, suggesting that joy is fleeting and bound to deeper spiritual quests.

Romantic literature often portrays happiness as existing beyond the material world, attainable only through imagination, nature, or love. However, this happiness is frequently accompanied by melancholy and the recognition of its impermanence, reflecting the Romantic preoccupation with the sublime and the ineffable.

X.3 Realism and the pursuit of practical happiness

In the Realist period of the mid-to-late 19th century, German literature shifted towards portraying everyday life and the social conditions that shape human experience. Writers like Theodor Fontane and Gottfried Keller explored the complexities of happiness within bourgeois society, focusing on personal relationships, duty, and societal expectations.

Fontane's *Effi Briest* highlights the constraints of social norms on individual happiness, illustrating how personal desires often clash with rigid structures. In contrast, Keller's *Green Henry (Der grüne Heinrich)* presents a more hopeful vision, suggesting that perseverance and self-awareness can lead to contentment, even in the face of disappointment.

X.4 Existentialism and the questioning of happiness

In the 20th century, existentialist and modernist German literature questioned the very foundation of happiness. Writers like Franz Kafka, Thomas Mann, and Hermann Hesse grappled with alienation, existential dread, and the search for meaning in an increasingly fragmented world. Kafka's works, such as *The Metamorphosis (Die Verwandlung),* depict protagonists trapped in absurd and oppressive circumstances, challenging the notion of happiness as an attainable goal.

Hesse's *Steppenwolf* delves into the psychological turmoil of its protagonist, suggesting that happiness requires reconciling the dualities within oneself. Similarly, Mann's *The Magic Mountain (Der Zauberberg)* explores the tension between hedonism and responsibility, portraying happiness as a complex and often elusive state.

X.5 Contemporary reflections on happiness

In contemporary German literature, happiness continues to be a multifaceted theme, reflecting issues such as migration, identity, and societal change. Authors like Jenny Erpenbeck and Daniel Kehlmann explore personal and collective happiness within the context of history, memory, and cultural upheaval. Erpenbeck's *Go, Went, Gone (Gehen, ging, gegangen)* examines the search for fulfillment in a world marked by displacement and uncertainty, while Kehlmann's *Measuring the World (Die Vermessung der Welt)* revisits Enlightenment ideals through the lives of historical figures.

Chapter XI
Happiness in Russian literature

The concept of happiness in Russian literature is a profound and multifaceted theme, reflecting the nation's cultural, historical, and philosophical currents. Unlike Western literary traditions that often portray happiness as a pursuit of individual fulfillment and external success, Russian literature frequently explores happiness through the lenses of suffering, morality, and existential qustioning.

XI.1 The roots of happiness in Russian literature

In Russian literature, happiness is rarely depicted as a simple or easily attainable state. Instead, it is often intertwined with spiritual or moral growth. The roots of this perspective can be traced to the deep influence of Orthodox Christianity, which emphasizes humility, compassion, and the redemptive power of suffering. Writers such as Fyodor Dostoevsky and Leo Tolstoy depict happiness as emerging from the ability to transcend personal ego and find meaning in service to others or alignment with higher moral principles.

XI.1.1 Dostoevsky: Happiness through suffering

Fyodor Dostoevsky's works are emblematic of the Russian literary focus on suffering as a path to happiness. In novels such as *Crime and Punishment* and *The Brothers Karamazov,* characters undergo intense psychological and moral struggles, with the possibility of happiness arising only through redemption and spiritual awakening. Dostoevsky suggests that happiness is not the absence of pain but rather the acceptance and transcendence of suffering. For Dostoevsky, love, forgiveness, and faith are essential to achieving true happiness.

XI.1.2 Tolstoy: Happiness in simplicity and moral clarity

Leo Tolstoy presents a different but complementary view of happiness, grounded in simplicity and the rejection of materialism. In *War and Peace* and *Anna Karenina,* Tolstoy contrasts the fleeting pleasures of high society with the enduring contentment found in familial love, rural life, and ethical living. His later philosophical writings, such as *The Kingdom of God is Within You,* argue that happiness stems from inner peace and adherence to moral and spiritual truths. Tolstoy's vision of happiness is deeply connected to a life of honesty, compassion, and alignment with nature.

XI.1.3 Chekhov: Fleeting happiness and the beauty of the moment

Anton Chekhov's short stories and plays often portray happiness as ephemeral and bittersweet. His characters experience moments of joy, love, and connection, yet these instances are transient, overshadowed by the inevitability of change and loss. In works such as *The Cherry Orchard* and *The Lady with the Dog,* happiness exists in small, fleeting moments that acquire poignancy precisely because they are impermanent. Chekhov's portrayal of happiness reflects a nuanced understanding of human fragility and the quiet beauty of ordinary life.

XI.2 Modern Soviet literature: The search for collective happiness

In the 20th century, Russian literature reflects broader social and political transformations. Soviet-era literature often emphasizes collective happiness, aligning personal fulfillment with the goals of the state and the broader collective.

Soviet literature emerged as a tool of state ideology, heavily influenced by the principles of Marxism-Leninism. Writers were encouraged—if not compelled—to align their narratives with the goals of socialism, which envisioned collective happiness achieved through the eradication of class distinctions and the establishment of a utopian society.

XI.2.1 Maxim Gorky and socialist realism

As a pioneer of socialist realism, Gorky's works often depict characters who find personal fulfillment through service to the collective. For example, his novel *Mother* portrays the protagonist's transformation as she embraces revolutionary ideals, suggesting that true happiness arises from collective struggle and unity.

XI.2.2 Mikhail Sholokhov's And Quiet Flows the Don

Sholokhov grapples with the complexities of individual and collective identities during the Russian Revolution and Civil War. His portrayal of Cossack life illustrates the sacrifices demanded by collective happiness, often leading to tragic consequences for individuals caught in the tide of history.

XI.2.3 The dissenting voices

Dissident writers challenged the Soviet ideal of collective happiness, arguing that it often masked systemic oppression. Aleksandr Solzhenitsyn's *One Day in the Life of Ivan Denisovich* offers a stark portrayal of life in a labor camp, emphasizing the dignity and inner strength of individuals even in the face of dehumanizing collectivism.

XI.2.4 Human spirit vs. state control

Writers like Andrei Platonov explored the contradictions inherent in the Soviet quest for utopia. His novel *The Foundation Pit* satirizes the blind pursuit of ideological goals at the expense of human lives, exposing the fragility of the collective happiness narrative.

XI.3 Broader implications

Both modern and Soviet literature grapple with the tension between individual autonomy and collective well-being. While some works celebrate the ideal of shared happiness, others highlight its potential for coercion and erasure of personal freedoms.

Chapter XII
Happiness in Arabic literature

The concept of happiness in Arabic literature is deeply intertwined with philosophical, spiritual, and poetic traditions. Across the ages, happiness was not merely seen as an emotional state but as a profound alignment of the self with divine, moral, and intellectual pursuits.

XII.1 Spiritual happiness in Sufi literature

Sufi poets and mystics like Rumi, Ibn Arabi, and Al-Ghazali saw happiness as union with God.

Al-Ghazali in his work *Ihyāʾ ʿulūm al-dīn* (The Revival of Religious Sciences) argued that true happiness lies in the purification of the heart and detachment from worldly desires.

For Sufis, happiness (sometimes expressed as wajd or ecstasy) is the result of divine love and experiencing the presence of the Beloved (God).

XII.2 Happiness in Arabic poetry and literature

In classical Arabic poetry (e.g., by Al-Mutanabbi, Abu Nuwas, and Al-Ma'arri), happiness often revolves around love, friendship, wine, and nature.

Poets like Abu Nuwas celebrated hedonistic pleasures as forms of transient happiness,[13] contrasting with the deeper spiritual happiness sought by Sufis.

Al-Ma'arri, on the other hand, expressed skepticism and believed that true happiness might be found in renouncing worldly life altogether.

XII.3 Happiness in Modern Arabic literature

Modern Arab writers like Naguib Mahfouz, Taha Hussein, and Khalil Gibran explore happiness as a complex negotiation between personal fulfillment, societal expectations, and existential struggles.

Gibran in *The Prophet* presents happiness as intertwined with sorrow – a holistic view that reflects the duality of human existence.

XII.4 *Key themes in the Arabic conceptions of happiness*

* *Divine connection* – Happiness as nearness to God.

* *Moral and intellectual growth* – True happiness stems from knowledge and virtue.

* *Ephemeral joys* – Happiness in fleeting worldly experiences (often with a melancholic undertone).

* *Community and love* – Happiness through relationships and shared experiences.

---

[13] See e.g. my books Åkesson, *An Unconventional Lover's Poetry: Abu Nuwas, 2025* and *Abu Nuwas: Selected Poems of Love, Wine and Life, 2025.*

Chapter XIII
Happiness in Japanese literature

The concept of happiness in Japanese literature is deeply interwoven with cultural, philosophical, and historical influences, evolving across different periods while reflecting Japan's unique aesthetic and spiritual sensibilities.

XIII.1 Classical period: Harmony with nature and ephemeral beauty

In the classical period, particularly during the Heian era (794–1185), happiness was often linked to the appreciation of natural beauty, harmony, and emotional refinement. Works like *The Tale of Genji* by Murasaki Shikibu explore the fleeting nature of joy and love, emphasizing the impermanence of human experiences. This ephemerality is tied to the concept of mono no aware, a deep, empathetic appreciation of the transience of things, where happiness and sadness coexist.

Poetry, especially in the Manyoshu and later in waka collections, also reflects happiness as moments of connection with nature or loved ones. Happiness is not portrayed as a permanent state but as a fleeting sensation, often accompanied by a melancholic awareness of its impermanence.

XIII.2 Medieval period: Spiritual transcendence and acceptance

In the medieval period (1185–1603), influenced by Zen Buddhism and Pure Land Buddhism, happiness was often defined in spiritual terms. This era's literature, such as *The Pillow Book* by Sei Shonagon or works like *Hojoki* by Kamo no Chomei, reflects themes of simplicity, detachment, and inner peace.

Zen-inspired poetry and prose emphasize mindfulness and contentment with the present moment. Happiness arises from spiritual enlightenment, acceptance of life's uncertainties, and the shedding of material desires. This outlook aligns with the Buddhist teachings on impermanence and suffering, where true happiness transcends worldly attachments.

XIII.3 Edo period: Everyday pleasures and the floating world

During the Edo period (1603–1868), happiness took on a more hedonistic and materialistic flavor, influenced by the prosperity of the merchant class. The literature of the *ukiyo* (floating world), such as Ihara Saikaku's works *(The Life of an Amorous Man),* often portrays happiness as the enjoyment of life's pleasures, whether through romantic escapades, food, or art.

In contrast, the haiku and tanka of Basho and other poets celebrate simple joys found in everyday life—listening to a frog jump into a pond or watching the blossoms fall. The aesthetic concept of *wabi-sabi,* which is centered on the acceptance of transience and imperfection., also underscores a quieter, understated form of happiness.

XIII.4 Modern period: Individuality, conflict, and hope

In the modern era *(Meiji* period onward), Japanese literature grapples with the complexities of happiness in an increasingly industrialized, globalized, and war-torn society. Writers like Natsume Soseki *(Kokoro)* and Junichiro Tanizaki *(Some Prefer Nettles*) examine the tension between traditional values and modern desires, often portraying happiness as elusive or fractured.

Post-World War II literature, including works by Yasunari Kawabata and Haruki Murakami, explores existential questions, disconnection, and the search for meaning in contemporary society. Happiness, in these narratives, is often portrayed as deeply personal and tied to self-discovery or fleeting moments of connection amid chaos.

XIII.5 Contemporary perspectives: Fragmentation and globalization

In contemporary Japanese literature, happiness is depicted in diverse and fragmented ways, reflecting modern life's complexities. Authors like Banana Yoshimoto *(Kitchen)* and Sayaka Murata *(Convenience Store Woman)* explore unconventional definitions of happiness through themes of individuality, alienation, and societal expectations.

The rise of globalized culture and environmental concerns has also influenced the depiction of happiness, often blending traditional Japanese sensibilities with modern existential dilemmas.

Chapter XIV
Happiness in Chinese literature

The concept of happiness in Chinese literature is deeply intertwined with philosophical, cultural, and historical influences. Over centuries, the portrayal of happiness has evolved, reflecting the values and ideals of different eras. Broadly, happiness in Chinese literature can be understood through three key lenses: Confucianism, Daoism, and Buddhism, each contributing distinct interpretations of what constitutes a fulfilling and joyful life.

XIV.1 Confucian perspective: Harmonious relationships and duty

Confucianism, which has profoundly shaped Chinese literature, emphasizes happiness as the result of fulfilling one's social roles and obligations. In classic texts like *The Analects* by Confucius, happiness is tied to ethical living, filial piety, and the cultivation of virtues such as benevolence *(ren)* and righteousness *(yi)*. Literature influenced by Confucian ideals often depicts happiness as the product of harmonious family relationships, loyalty to one's country, and contributing to societal well-being.

For example, in classical novels like *Dream of the Red Chamber (红楼梦)* by Cao Xueqin, happiness is frequently portrayed through the lens of familial bonds and personal sacrifice. Even as characters pursue romantic or material desires, true happiness is often framed as the restoration of social harmony and the fulfillment of one's responsibilities.

XIV.2 Daoist perspective: Simplicity and natural harmony

Daoist literature, on the other hand, presents a more introspective and nature-oriented view of happiness. Texts like *Dao De Jing* (道德经) by Laozi emphasize the importance of living in harmony with the Dao (the Way), suggesting that happiness comes from simplicity, spontaneity, and non-attachment. Daoist poetry and prose often celebrate the beauty of nature, solitude, and a life unburdened by material concerns or societal expectations.

Poets like Li Bai (李白) and Tao Yuanming (陶渊明) epitomize this perspective. In their works, happiness is portrayed as found in rustic life, wandering through mountains, drinking wine, and immersing oneself in the natural world. Tao Yuanming's poem *Return to the Fields* (归园田居) exemplifies the Daoist ideal of retreating to rural life, finding joy in simplicity and self-sufficiency.

XIV.3 Buddhist perspective: Inner peace and enlightenment

Buddhism adds another layer to the literary portrayal of happiness. Buddhist literature often reflects on the transient nature of life and the suffering that arises from attachment and desire. Happiness, from this viewpoint, is found in inner peace, compassion, and the pursuit of enlightenment.

Works like *Journey to the West* (西游记) by Wu Cheng'en blend Buddhist teachings with adventure and humor, illustrating how characters achieve happiness by overcoming ego and ignorance. The journey of the monk Xuanzang and his companions serves as an allegory for the spiritual quest for enlightenment, suggesting that happiness ultimately lies in self-realization and the alleviation of suffering.

XIV.4 Folk traditions and popular literature: Celebration and everyday joy

Beyond philosophical texts, Chinese folk tales and popular literature reflect a more immediate and communal sense of happiness. Stories of mythical immortals, celebrations of festivals, and the joy found in daily life highlight a culturally grounded and vibrant understanding of happiness. Traditional festivals such as the Mid-Autumn Festival, celebrated in countless poems and stories, emphasize reunion, abundance, and the joy of shared experience.

XIV.5 Modern and contemporary reflections

In modern Chinese literature, happiness often intersects with themes of personal freedom, love, and the search for identity in the face of social change. Writers like Lu Xun (鲁迅) explore the complexities of modern life, sometimes portraying happiness as elusive yet still tied to resilience and hope.

Ultimately, happiness in Chinese literature reflects a rich tapestry of philosophical inquiry, personal reflection, and cultural celebration. Whether through Confucian ideals of duty, Daoist reverence for nature, or Buddhist quests for enlightenment, Chinese literary works offer diverse yet interconnected visions of what it means to live a fulfilled life.

Chapter XV:
Happiness in art

Happiness can be explored and expressed through various art forms. Each medium provides a unique way to represent and evoke joy, contentment, and positivity. By combining creativity with an understanding of human emotions, artists can evoke joy and positivity in powerful ways.

XV.1 Happiness in painting

Happiness in painting is a universal yet deeply personal theme that transcends cultural and historical boundaries. Artists have long sought to capture the essence of joy, contentment, and serenity through various forms, from the vibrant brushstrokes of Impressionism to the symbolic storytelling of contemporary installations.

XV.1.1 Color and emotion

Bright, saturated colors like yellows, oranges, and pinks are often used to evoke feelings of warmth and happiness. Artists such as Henri Matisse and Vincent van Gogh used dynamic color palettes to channel joy and hope, even in difficult times.

XV.1.2 Subject matter

Scenes of celebration, nature, human connection, and leisure often symbolize happiness. Impressionists like Renoir painted bustling social gatherings, while Romanticists highlighted the sublime beauty of the natural world.

XV.1.3 Abstract representations, symbolism and metaphor, contemporary installations

Modern and abstract artists explore happiness through shape, movement, and form. Wassily Kandinsky's compositions reflect the harmony and rhythm that can mirror emotional uplift.

Objects such as blooming flowers, sunlight, and open landscapes serve as metaphors for contentment. Contemporary artists might use symbols like balloons, kites, or dancing figures to convey lightness and freedom.

Contemporary installations invite viewers to engage with art physically, creating immersive environments that spark happiness. Yayoi Kusama's mirrored infinity rooms evoke wonder and delight, while large-scale public installations foster communal joy.

XV.1.4 Cultural interpretations

Different cultures express happiness in unique visual languages. Japanese ukiyo-e prints celebrate fleeting moments of pleasure, while African tribal art may depict dance and communal festivities.

XV.2 The power of art to evoke happiness

Art has the ability not only to depict happiness but to generate it in viewers. This emotional resonance creates a feedback loop—art inspires joy, which in turn influences the way we see the world.

XV.2.1 Impressionism – The joy of everyday life

Artists: Pierre-Auguste Renoir, Claude Monet, Edgar Degas

Impressionists sought to capture fleeting moments of light and life. Renoir's *"Luncheon of the Boating Party"* portrays people enjoying food, drink, and companionship by the riverside, embodying simple pleasures and social joy.

Monet's garden paintings, such as *"Water Lilies"*, create a serene, immersive experience, using color and light to reflect tranquility and contentment.

**Key elements:* Soft brushstrokes, vibrant colors, and depictions of leisure and nature.

XV.2.2 Post-impressionism – Emotional radiance

Artists: Vincent van Gogh, Paul Gauguin

Van Gogh's *"Sunflowers"* and *"The Starry Night"* convey exuberance through swirling, dynamic brushwork and bright, radiant colors. Despite personal struggles, his work often reveals a longing for happiness and connection.

Gauguin's use of tropical settings, such as *"Tahitian Women on the Beach"*, evokes the joy of unspoiled nature and simplicity.

Key elements: Emotional intensity, bold colors, and symbolic landscapes.

XV.2.3 Fauvism – Pure expression of joy

Artists: Henri Matisse, André Derain

Fauvist painters, led by Matisse, used wild, unnatural colors and bold patterns to express happiness. Matisse's *"The Dance"* celebrates movement, freedom, and communal joy, while *"The Red Room"* creates a warm, inviting interior.

Key elements: Non-naturalistic color, expressive forms, and simplified shapes.

XV.2.4 Surrealism – Dreamlike bliss

Artists: Joan Miró, Salvador Dalí

Miró's abstract compositions, such as *"The Garden"*, use whimsical shapes and playful colors to evoke childlike happiness and the subconscious's boundless creativity.

Key elements: Dream imagery, imaginative forms, and playful abstraction.

XV.2.5 Contemporary and interactive art – Shared joy

Artists: Yayoi Kusama, Olafur Eliasson, Banksy

Kusama's *Infinity Mirror Rooms* surround viewers with endless reflections of light and pattern, inducing awe and wonder.

Eliasson's *"The Weather Project"* (a large sun installation) filled the Tate Modern with a glowing light that transformed the space into a communal haven of warmth.

Key elements: Immersive environments, public engagement, and large-scale installations.

XV.2.6 Folk and cultural art – Celebrating traditions

Mexican Día de los Muertos art celebrates life and remembrance with bright colors and smiling skeleton figures.

Indian Rangoli and Madhubani paintings feature intricate, joyful patterns that honor festivals and familial bonds.

XV.3 Happiness in music

The concept of happiness in music is a rich and multifaceted concept that spans emotional, cultural, psychological, and even physiological dimensions. Music has the power to evoke and amplify happiness, serving as both a mirror and a catalyst for joyful experiences.

XV.3.1 Emotional expression and connection

* *Music as a mood enhancer:* Uplifting melodies, bright harmonies, and fast tempos often evoke feelings of happiness. Songs in major keys with catchy, rhythmic patterns are commonly associated with joy and celebration.

* *Emotional release:* Music can serve as a conduit for processing emotions, allowing listeners to release tension, reminisce about joyful memories, or experience pure euphoria.

* *Shared experience:* Festivals, concerts, and communal singing amplify happiness by creating a collective sense of belonging and shared joy.

XV.3.2 Cultural significance of joy in music

* *Celebratory traditions:* Cultures around the world use music in rituals and ceremonies to express happiness — from wedding dances to religious hymns to victory songs.

* *Genres of joy:* Different musical genres encapsulate happiness uniquely. For example:

* *Pop* – Catchy, light-hearted tunes with positive lyrics.

* *Afrobeat/Reggae* – Rhythms that inspire movement and a sense of freedom.

* *Classical* – Symphonic pieces with uplifting, soaring melodies (e.g., Beethoven's 9th Symphony).

XV.3.3 Psychological and physiological impact

* *Release of dopamine:* Listening to music activates brain regions associated with pleasure, such as the nucleus accumbens, triggering the release of dopamine – the "feel-good" neurotransmitter.

* *Stress reduction:* Happy music can reduce cortisol levels, alleviating stress and promoting overall well-being.

* *Memory and nostalgia:* Songs tied to positive memories can trigger happiness by transporting listeners to joyful moments in their past.

XV.4 Creative expression of happiness in composition

XV.4.1 Musical techniques

* *Key signatures and scales:* Major scales, pentatonic melodies, and consonant harmonies often evoke happiness.

**Instruments and timbre:* Bright-sounding instruments like trumpets, violins, and pianos are often associated with joyous music.

**Rhythm and tempo:* Upbeat, fast tempos (120 bpm or higher) naturally energize and uplift listeners.

XV.4.2 Examples of happiness in music

* *"Don't Stop Me Now"* by Queen – High energy, empowering lyrics, and dynamic instrumentation.
* *"Here Comes the Sun"* by The Beatles – Gentle, optimistic tone with bright guitar riffs.
* *"Happy"* by Pharrell Williams – Explicitly crafted to embody the feeling of joy through its simple, catchy structure and lyrics.

XV.4.3 The role of music in mental health and therapy

* *Music therapy:* Used to enhance mood and treat depression, with carefully selected joyful songs to improve patients' emotional states.
* *Personalized playlists:* People often curate playlists that reflect their happiest moments, creating a go-to source for positivity.

XV.5 Happiness in dance

The idea of happiness in dance is a rich and multifaceted concept that can be explored through various lenses—psychological, cultural, philosophical, and artistic.

XV.5.1 Physical expression of joy

Dance is one of the most primal forms of human expression. The body's movement in sync with rhythm often mirrors feelings of joy, liberation, and celebration. From folk dances to spontaneous movement at a party, dance serves as a universal language of happiness.

* *Endorphins and movement:* Scientifically, dancing stimulates the release of endorphins, reducing stress and boosting mood.

* *Freestyle dance:* In forms like street dance or contemporary freestyle, dancers express personal happiness through fluid, uninhibited movements.

XV.5.2 Cultural and ritualistic dance

Across cultures, dance is embedded in ceremonies, festivals, and communal gatherings.

* *Celebratory dances:* Salsa, samba, bhangra, and other traditional dances celebrate harvests, weddings, and milestones.

* *Spiritual ecstasy:* In many cultures, dance serves as a connection to the divine, producing feelings of bliss (e.g., Sufi whirling, African trance dances).

XV.5.3 Dance as a personal journey

For many, dance is a tool for personal healing and self-discovery. Dance therapy uses movement to enhance mental health and foster emotional resilience.

* *Flow state:* Psychologist Mihaly Csikszentmihalyi's concept of "flow" often applies to dance. When dancers enter this state, they experience deep immersion and joy.

* *Mind-body connection:* Dance brings awareness to the body, grounding individuals in the present moment, similar to mindfulness.

XV.5.4 Social bonding and community

Dancing in groups, whether in a class or on the dance floor, creates social connections. Shared movement fosters camaraderie, belonging, and collective joy.

* *Flash mobs and group dances:* Events where people dance together foster collective euphoria and unity.

XV.5.5 Performance and artistic fulfillment

Professional dancers often describe the stage as a place of transcendence and fulfillment. The joy of perfecting choreography or improvising onstage fuels passion.

**Artistic catharsis:* Dance as performance allows for emotional release, connecting with audiences and generating shared joy.

XV.5.6 Everyday happiness through dance

Dance doesn't have to be formal. Dancing alone in a room, moving while cooking, or dancing with family can be small yet powerful acts of happiness.

In essence, happiness in dance transcends technique or form—it lies in the freedom, community, and connection that movement brings. Whether performed professionally or casually, dance offers a profound pathway to joy and self-expression.

XV.6 Happiness in theatre

The idea of happiness in theatre is deeply multifaceted, as theatre reflects the complexities of human emotions and experiences. Happiness, as portrayed in theatre, can range from moments of pure joy and celebration to a pursuit of meaning and fulfillment amidst adversity. This exploration often serves as a vehicle for both entertainment and introspection.

XV.6.1 Classical theater

In ancient Greek tragedies and comedies, happiness was often tied to fate and the gods' will. For example, in Aristophanes' comedies, happiness is depicted humorously, often as relief from societal pressures or personal struggles.

Tragedies like Sophocles' *Oedipus Rex* showcase happiness as fragile, with characters experiencing moments of joy only to face dramatic reversals.

XV.6.2 Renaissance theater

Shakespeare explored happiness through themes of love, power, and identity. Comedies like *A Midsummer Night's Dream* portray happiness as a resolution to romantic and social conflicts, while tragedies like Hamlet question whether true happiness is attainable.

XV.6.3 Modern and postmodern theater

Modern playwrights like Chekhov and Ibsen often present happiness as elusive, tied to existential struggles and societal expectations. In contrast, postmodern plays might critique the idea of happiness altogether, focusing instead on irony and fragmented narratives.

XV.6.4 Happiness as celebration

Many theatrical works use joy and celebration to evoke happiness, often in the form of music, dance, and comedic situations. These moments can offer audiences an escape or a sense of shared delight.

Example: "Mamma Mia!"

The musical uses upbeat ABBA songs and lively choreography to create an atmosphere of sheer joy. The story itself centers on themes of love, family, and the pursuit of happiness, culminating in celebratory moments that engage the audience.

Example: Shakespeare's Comedies

Plays like *A Midsummer Night's Dream* and *As You Like It* often end with joyous weddings or reunions, symbolizing harmony and happiness.

* *Twelfth Night* (Shakespeare) – Happiness achieved through love and mistaken identities

XV.6.5 Happiness as the pursuit of fulfillment

Theatre often portrays characters striving for happiness, highlighting the challenges and sacrifices involved in achieving it. This approach emphasizes that happiness is not just an emotional state but a journey.

Example: "Death of a Salesman" by Arthur Miller

Willy Loman's pursuit of the American dream reflects a misguided quest for happiness tied to material success and societal validation. The play examines how this pursuit can lead to disillusionment, suggesting a more profound, introspective understanding of happiness.

**Example:* "Fiddler on the Roof" by Joseph Stein*

Tevye's struggle to balance tradition with the happiness of his daughters reveals the complexities of finding joy in a changing world.

XV.6.6 Happiness in adversity

Some plays depict moments of happiness amidst adversity, underscoring human resilience and the power of joy even in dark times.

**Example:* "Les Misérables" by Victor Hugo*

While much of the story is marked by hardship, moments like Cosette and Marius's love symbolize hope and happiness emerging from despair.

**Example:* "The Diary of Anne Frank" by Frances Goodrich and Albert Hackett*

Despite the grim circumstances, Anne's unwavering optimism and moments of laughter shared among the characters serve as powerful reminders of the human capacity for joy.

XV.6.7 Happiness as illusion or satire

Theatre also questions and critiques conventional notions of happiness, often using satire to reveal its fragility or superficiality.

**Example:* "Candide" by Voltaire (adapted for theatre by Leonard Bernstein)*

This satirical operetta mocks the overly optimistic philosophy of *"everything happens for the best,"* portraying a naive protagonist's search for happiness in a harsh world.

* *Example: "Waiting for Godot" by Samuel Beckett*

Beckett's absurdist play challenges traditional concepts of happiness by showing characters clinging to hope and finding fleeting moments of humor in an otherwise bleak and uncertain existence.

XV.6.8 Happiness as community and connection

Theatre often depicts happiness as arising from relationships and shared experiences, emphasizing the importance of community.

* *Example: "Our Town" by Thornton Wilder*

The play highlights the beauty of everyday life and the happiness found in simple, meaningful connections with others.

* *Example: "Come From Away" by Irene Sankoff and David Hein*

This musical portrays the kindness and solidarity of a small town welcoming stranded travelers during a crisis, showing happiness as a collective and compassionate experience.

www.ingramcontent.com/pod-product-compliance
Ingram Content Group UK Ltd.
Pitfield, Milton Keynes, MK11 3LW, UK
UKHW012253290726
14090UKWH00016B/617

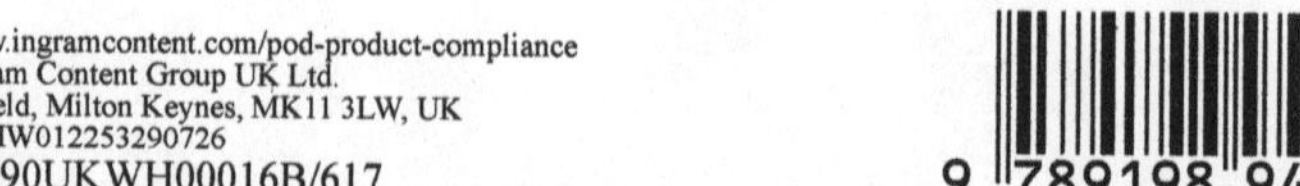

9 789198 945423